Joy Together

Joy Together

Spiritual Practices
for Your Congregation

LYNNE M. BAAB

WESTMINSTER
JOHN KNOX PRESS
LOUISVILLE · KENTUCKY

© 2012 Lynne M. Baab

First edition
Published by Westminster John Knox Press
Louisville, Kentucky

12 13 14 15 16 17 18 19 20 21 — 10 9 8 7 6 5 4 3 2 1

Scripture quotations from the New Revised Standard Version of the Bible are copyright © 1989 by the Division of Christian Education of the National Council of the Churches of Christ in the U.S.A. and are used by permission.

Prayer used in worship at Westminster College, Cambridge, United Kingdom, was written by Susan Durber, Principal. The fourth line comes from the title of a book by David Cornick, *Letting God Be God: The Reformed Tradition* (Maryknoll, NY: Orbis Books, 2008). Used with permission of Susan Durber.

All stories are told with permission. Names of individuals and churches have been changed, as well as some identifying details.

Book design by Drew Stevens
Cover design by Dilu Nicholas
Cover art © melhi / istockphoto.com

Library of Congress Cataloging-in-Publication Data
Baab, Lynne M.
    Joy together : spiritual practices for your congregation / Lynne M. Baab.
        p. cm.
    ISBN 978-0-664-23709-7 (alk. paper)
    1. Spiritual life. I. Title.
BV4501.3.B325 2012
248.4'6—dc23
                                                                        2012011845

♾ The paper used in this publication meets the minimum requirements of the American National Standard for Information Sciences — Permanence of Paper for Printed Library Materials, ANSI Z39.48-1992

Most Westminster John Knox Press books are available at special quantity discounts when purchased in bulk by corporations, organizations, and special-interest groups. For more information, please e-mail SpecialSales@wjkbooks.com.

CONTENTS

ACKNOWLEDGMENTS

When I write a book, I interview dozens of people by phone and e-mail and in person. The interviews stimulate my thinking in multiple ways, and I know I couldn't write books without the engagement and exchange that come through the interviews. I often feel like I'm cheating when I write because I'm using thoughts that come from friends and colleagues. It doesn't seem fair that I get credit as the author when my ideas come from conversations with so many other people. When I said exactly that to one of my interviewees, she responded by saying that my interview/writing method illustrates the main point of the book: that doing things communally is richer and more rewarding than doing them alone. What a lovely and relevant observation!

During the preparation time and the writing of this book, numerous people made comments in casual conversations that stimulated my thoughts. Thank you, friends and colleagues, for being such interesting people to talk to and for getting me thinking about so many aspects of the Christian life.

A number of people gave me an hour or more for an interview about the topics in this book. Many thanks to these friends and colleagues for giving me your time and your thoughts: Rev. Dan Baumgartner, Rev. Steve Lympus, Rev. Rebecca Blackwell, Connie Anderson, Rev. Mark Johnston, Rev. Henry Mbambo, Dr. Susan Phillips, Sister Dorothy Eggering, Tara Taylor, Tim Keel, Rev. Merrie Carson, and Rev. Doug Early.

Other people wrote me e-mails or letters that laid out their experiences with communal spiritual disciplines. A warm thank you to Jane Pelz, Dianne Ross, Paddy Payne, Carey Berend, Jeff Brooks, Jordan Kleber, Rev. Colin Morrison, Joanne Wardle, Rev. Renee Sundberg, Lisa Jeremiah, Rev. Peter Hughes, Suzanne Gilman, and Sue Suneson.

Several people helped me find quotations for the sidebars, and I want to thank them: Tara Taylor, Kimberlee Conway Ireton, Carol Simon, and Steve Lympus. Special thanks to Priscilla Atkins and Lezlie Gruenler at Hope College, who helped me find citations for quotations.

Rev. Geoff New interacted significantly with me about the topics of this book, gave me feedback on an early version of one chapter, and helped me find quotations for the sidebars. He also helped me find resources on *lectio divina* and Ignatian Gospel Contemplation, and his Doctor of Ministry thesis stimulated my thinking a great deal. Margie Van Duzer also interacted with me about the topics of this book and gave me helpful feedback on an early version of one chapter. She allowed me to read her Doctor of Ministry thesis, which helped me clarify my thoughts about one section of this book.

My thanks to Andrew Shepherd, who recommended readings for the hospitality chapter and whose PhD thesis stimulated my thinking about hospitality.

During the writing of this book I attended a seminar on the missional church led by Alan Roxburgh. Many of his ideas influenced my thoughts as I wrote, and I am indebted to him for his contagious passion for vibrant congregations.

A special thanks to Dr. David Stubbs, Professor of Ethics and Theology at Western Theological Seminary in

Holland, Michigan, who talked to me at length about the ways that following Jesus is and is not a practice, giving me foundational ideas for chapter 9. David also read the chapter in its early stages and made suggestions for shaping it.

Warm thanks to Dr. Paul Trebilco and Rev. Merrie Carson, who also read sections of this book in early forms and helped me refine it.

My editor at Westminster John Knox Press, Jana Riess, made many valuable suggestions to refine my thoughts and help me express myself better. Thank you, Jana, for giving me the gift of your insight and perception.

Many of my most significant experiences of communal spiritual disciplines are linked with my husband, Dave. Together we have kept the Sabbath, prayed in countless ways and settings, and participated in a wide variety of Christian spiritual practices in small groups and congregations. Thank you, Dave, for being the best imaginable soul partner.

1

DISCIPLINE? NO THANKS!

I appeal to you therefore, brothers and sisters, by the mercies of God, to present your bodies as a living sacrifice, holy and acceptable to God, which is your spiritual worship. Do not be conformed to this world, but be transformed by the renewing of your minds, so that you may discern what is the will of God— what is good and acceptable and perfect.
— Romans 12:1–2

During the summer of 2005, I heard dozens of stories about fasting. I learned why and how Christians fast. Some people told me why they don't fast, and expressed their questions and concerns.

I sought out all the interviews because I was writing a book about fasting. I had fasted numerous times; I read books about fasting and heard stories from a few friends about their fasts, so I was confident I could write a good book. But I knew I needed more stories before I could start writing, so I sent out an e-mail to just about every person I knew, asking for stories or referrals to friends of theirs who fasted.

The return e-mails poured in. Many more of my acquaintances fast than I had realized, and some fast quite frequently. Many of them do it secretly, seeking to obey the words of Jesus in Matthew 6:16–17 where he talks about fasting in such a way as to be seen only by God. This explains why I didn't know they fasted.

I was surprised by the number of people who fast, but what surprised me even more was the number of people who fast with others. Husbands and wives. Parents and grown children. Extended families who are praying for a family member in need. Small groups. Whole congregations. I was amazed, because I had always fasted alone.

Some of my friends gave me contact information for their friends in Africa, Asia, and South America, where communal fasting often plays a significant role in congregational life. Those Christians told me that they interpret Jesus' words in Matthew 6 to mean that the motive of fasting matters. We must not fast to impress people, they said, but to please God. Their congregations announce weekly or monthly fast days with lists of prayer requests for the fasts, and in times of special need they fast for a week at a time or longer. They experience God's presence in special ways when they fast communally, and the joy and power of communal fasting is so clear to them that they couldn't understand why many westerners fast all alone.

The communal nature of the fasts described by my interviewees got me thinking. For many years, my husband and I observed the Sabbath with our children. Our Sabbaths were communal in the sense that our nuclear family engaged in the Sabbath together, but we never considered connecting with other families who were doing the same thing. I experienced contemplative prayer in groups, and I loved the group experience of quiet prayer. However, when I reflected on "spiritual disciplines" or "spiritual practices" (terms that I will use interchangeably in this book), I mostly thought about doing something that would help me as an individual to draw near to God in the privacy of my own metaphorical prayer closet.

The stories I heard about fasting helped me start paying attention to communal spiritual practices. This book is the outgrowth of the pondering and listening I have engaged in since I wrote my book on fasting. I want to give groups of people—small groups, whole congregations, and other groups of Christians—models of spiritual disciplines that are experienced communally. I want to convey some of the richness of our Christian heritage; throughout the ages, in diverse settings, many Christians have engaged in spiritual practices with others. I want to transmit my enthusiasm for the ways communal spiritual disciplines can enrich Christian life and shape us into people who are not conformed to this world but are transformed increasingly into the image and likeness of Jesus. I want to communicate the ways that spiritual practices are richer—and usually easier—when we engage in them with others.

> *We delude ourselves if we imagine that we can live the spiritual life in total isolation from Christian community, for it is impossible to be Christian in solitary splendor.*
>
> —Marjorie J. Thompson, *Soul Feast*

Individuals and Communities

Most books on spiritual practices begin with the individual, and many individual Christians have found great benefit by engaging in personal spiritual disciplines. They have overcome an innate distaste for the word "discipline" and have come to understand a spiritual discipline as any practice that clears away the clutter of daily life and helps a person make space for God.

A renewed emphasis on Christian history has helped make the word "discipline" more palatable. Throughout most of the past two millennia, the disciplined actions connected to the Christian life were viewed as significant and transformative. In the modern period, with its emphasis on objective truth and scientific research, being a Christian was often viewed as assenting to a series of propositions about God. Now we are coming back to a renewed understanding that the way we live our lives—the actions we engage in as a response to God's love for us—matter as well. Spiritual disciplines give shape to our daily lives and help us experience God's presence in all of life. They help us respond to God's initiative. And they shape us.

In an age of consumerism, the word "discipline" has taken on additional significance. Decades of materialistic self-indulgence have vividly illustrated the Gospel reality that we "cannot serve God and wealth" and that life is "more than food, and the body more than clothing" (Matt. 6:24, 25). Spiritual disciplines are one way to engage with Jesus' admonition to seek first the kingdom of God and God's righteousness (Matt. 6:33).

> *The word discipline means "the effort to create some space in which God can act." Discipline means to prevent everything in your life from being filled up.*
>
> —Henri Nouwen, "Moving from Solitude to Community to Ministry"

With the rise in engagement with spiritual disciplines by individuals, many are beginning to ask if spiritual practices can be experienced in community as well. Doug, a Presbyterian minister who serves a large urban congregation, would answer "yes" with enthusiasm. "I have seen such value in people coming together to engage in spiritual practices," he reflected. "When we do things with others, it makes up for our own shortcomings.

It helps us think outside the box. It's easier to dream when you're encouraged and even pushed by someone else."

Doug frequently leads his elders in corporate spiritual practices. At the monthly session (board) meetings, he sets up a variety of different prayer experiences for the elders and pastoral staff so that they can pray in creative ways for the needs of the congregation and the wider community and so that they can listen to God. He wants to give people practice engaging in new forms of prayer in order for them to learn how to do it themselves. He believes that the church elders are living out their faith commitment in front of other people, allowing the prayer they engage in together to be their most important form of leadership. "This helps shape the group into a tighter knit community, and it helps them model to the large community they are leading, which picks up what the leaders are doing, a bit like osmosis."

Doug's congregation offers numerous options for learning about and experiencing a variety of spiritual disciplines, and he has seen the fruit of those opportunities in various ways: deepening faith, ability to hear God's voice, and willingness to serve. Communal spiritual disciplines also bring authenticity to a congregation's life. When people are meeting God in new ways, they talk about it. They experience God's guidance in challenging situations, the Holy Spirit's presence and comfort in the midst of crisis, and Jesus' peace that passes understanding. They receive God's love, and they pass it on to others. After all, if God is real, if Jesus really did live and die and then live

> *Taste and see that the LORD is good.*
>
> —Psalm 34:8

again, and if the Holy Spirit is truly present in us and with us, then any actions that reflect our commitment to follow Jesus will spill over into every sphere of life.

The practice of communal spiritual disciplines in congregations helps the leaders receive direction from God. In our time, with declining numbers in many congregations, congregations need to know exactly where God is calling them to serve in their wider community. In his prayer for believers on the night he was betrayed, Jesus says that we are sent into the world as he was sent into the world (John 17:18). Jesus modeled extended prayer times where he heard God's voice, directing him where to go and what to do (Mark 1:35–38). Christian spiritual disciplines help us make space in our lives so that we can pray and listen in a similar way.

What Exactly Are Spiritual Disciplines?

Three authors have shaped my understanding of what constitutes a spiritual discipline or spiritual practice. Each of these authors also provides lists that can help expand the options we can consider.

Marjorie Thompson, in her 1995 book *Soul Feast*, describes seven spiritual disciplines: reading of Scripture, prayer, worship, fasting, confession/self-examination, spiritual direction, and hospitality. She writes that her purpose is "to help people of faith understand and begin to practice some of the basic disciplines of the Christian spiritual life. Disciplines are simply practices that train us in faithfulness. . . . Such practices have consistently been experienced as vehicles of God's presence, guidance, and call in the lives of faithful seekers."[1] Thompson's definition, that disciplines are simply *practices*

> *What is discipline? Look at the word; there is no hint of punishment in it. A disciple is a follower, and discipline is the state of the follower, learner, imitator.*
>
> —Charlotte Mason,
> *Parents and Children*

that train us in faithfulness, illustrates the overlap of the two words "discipline" and "practices." To me, these two names mean the same thing.

But Thompson's seven practices are not the only ones to consider. Tony Jones, a leader of the North American emergent church movement, describes sixteen spiritual disciplines in his 2005 book, *The Sacred Way.* Jones includes most of the spiritual disciplines mentioned by Marjorie Thompson, and adds others such as pilgrimage, meditation, and the Jesus Prayer. Jones uses the analogy of learning to play a musical instrument or growing competent in a sport. Proficiency requires practice, he reflects:

> If there's a common theme among the great Christian spiritual writers, it's this: Seeking God will not be easy. The history of the church is the story of many faithful Christians admirably fighting back their own sins by these disciplines, only to be thwarted again and again. But, as with a sport, the more you practice, the better you get. You'll get in better "spiritual shape" as you practice, and you'll be able to run the race to completion.[2]

Jones's comparison of the Christian life to learning a sport or learning to play a musical instrument illuminates a profound truth. God is in the business of transforming us into the image of Jesus Christ (2 Cor. 3:18), and that transformation doesn't begin and end on the day we acknowledge Jesus as our Lord and Savior. That transformation continues over our entire lives, and we do indeed change as we "practice" living the Christian life.

Adele Ahlberg Calhoun describes more than sixty specific spiritual disciplines in her *Spiritual Disciplines Handbook,* also published in 2005. She includes many forms of prayer and Bible study, along with retreats, pilgrimages, and other actions that could be considered to be spiritual practices. Her list expands the possibilities for what exactly constitutes a spiritual discipline, and her definition is also helpful: "From its beginning, the church linked the desire for more of God to intentional practices, relationships, and experiences that gave people space in their lives to 'keep company' with Jesus. These intentional practices, relationships and experiences we know as *spiritual disciplines*."[3]

Calhoun's *Spiritual Disciplines Handbook*, by including so many different and specific spiritual disciplines, makes clear that many habits or practices in daily life can be considered spiritual disciplines. The mother who stands by the front door as her children leave in the morning and says a brief prayer for each child when the door closes is engaging in a practice that "trains her in faithfulness" and helps her "keep company with Jesus." In the same way, the man who has a habit of glancing at a Scripture verse on his iPhone when he waits for the elevator at work is being trained in faithfulness and is keeping company with Jesus. No one can possibly engage in sixty spiritual practices. In fact, most people cannot engage in more than a few, but a long list helps provide an overview of the options and helps us notice—and think creatively—about the things we already do that help us keep company with Jesus or that train us in faithfulness.

Spiritual practices don't need to be just for the individual. Sunday worship in congregations—with singing, prayers, the reading of Scripture, the preaching of the Word, the sacraments of baptism and Communion, and congregational fellowship afterward—enables worshipers to keep company with Jesus and provides training in faithfulness. So a practice of attending the worship service and engaging in the various components of worship can certainly be considered a spiritual discipline. Many congregational activities, such as prayer meetings, small-group Bible studies, and home prayer groups, can also be considered spiritual practices.

I view worship, small groups, and congregational fellowship as indispensable and essential to the Christian life, but I would also like to see congregations engage further in spiritual practices because I believe they bring depth and vitality. This book describes six specific spiritual disciplines in detail, with illustrations from congregations to show how these practices can be experienced communally. The six disciplines are:

— Thankfulness
— Fasting
— Contemplative prayer
— Contemplative approaches to Scripture
— Hospitality
— Sabbath keeping

These six were chosen because of my deep concerns for the Church of Jesus Christ in the affluent West, which I will discuss in the next section. I believe these six spiritual disciplines go a long way toward addressing several significant concerns, acting as a positive corrective to some of the forces at work in our lives today.

Some Challenges We Face

My first concern relates to consumerism and materialism. In North America, Europe, Australia, and New Zealand, where I live, as well as in many other countries, we are steeped in the advertising culture. Even if we try as hard as we can to resist the lure of material possessions, we are profoundly influenced by a consumer outlook. We need all the help we can get to remember God's priorities. The spiritual disciplines I have chosen, particularly when practiced communally, help us resist the attractions of acquiring an ever-increasing number of possessions. They help us rest in love, grace, and peace, which come from God alone.

My second concern about the church today comes from my conviction that all of us need to grow in our ability to experience God's guidance in our daily lives. The parents of a demanding teenager need help to know how to love and discipline their son or daughter in a way that will work best for that specific child. The project manager who feels overwhelmed by the task ahead needs help to know when to push the team and when to let up and celebrate the things that have been achieved. The apartment dweller who is losing sleep because of a noisy neighbor needs to know how best to approach the neighbor and the landlord. God, the source of all wisdom, surely knows the answers to these conundrums. But how do we tap God's wisdom? And how can we learn to do it with a pace of life that seems to accelerate every day?

Learning how to listen for God's voice in the midst of our challenges makes life richer and fuller, and it helps us understand that God cares about every aspect of our lives. God's voice comes to us in Scripture, giving us wisdom and guidance for daily life, rooted in the way we were created and the life we were made for. God's voice also comes to us from the nudging of the Holy Spirit within us, sometimes in response to a passage from the Bible, sometimes while engaging in various spiritual practices, and sometimes through our own conscience. We need to hear God's voice in all of these ways, and the spiritual practices described in this book help develop our ability to listen to God through Scripture and through the work of the Holy Spirit in us.

In addition to our concerns about our daily challenges and worries, we also need to hear God's voice about the contribution God wants us to make each day. For what purpose did God create me? What unique gifts, given to me by God, do I have to offer? Why am I here? We need God's guidance each day about how to become the people we were created to be and how to serve in this broken world. Spiritual disciplines, exercised individually and communally, help us receive answers from God to these big questions.

Congregations face similar vexing practical challenges and issues related to identity. Scenarios might include the following:

— Our congregation is having a shortfall in giving. Should we cut back on expenses or try to find other sources of money?
— We want to reach out to our neighborhood in some new ways. One group within the church is advocating for a project in the local school, while another group wants to host a food pantry. We can't do both. How do we know which one to do?
— And why are we here? What unique purpose does God have for us as a congregation? What gifts can we bring to the wider community?

All of the spiritual disciplines chosen for this book have a significant component of listening. These spiritual practices put us in a receptive place that trains us in listening to God and to others. Spiritual practices enable us to listen for God's answers to the specific issues we are facing, and they help us listen for God's voice leading us in entirely new directions. Sometimes we will discern God leading us into paths we have never considered.

My third concern for the church in the affluent West relates to the fact that in many instances we have lost our way as Christians called to be the church. This is closely connected to my first two concerns. Consumerism shuts down our ability to listen to God because we are so focused on the next possession or the next experience. When we do try to listen to God, we often find ourselves wrapped up primarily with our own concerns about

> *Where two or three are gathered in my name, I am there among them.*
>
> —Matthew 18:20

family, work, health, or other pressing issues. When we try to listen to God communally, again we often focus mostly on the pressing concerns of our church community. We tend to be consumers, even in the way we approach Christian life. We focus on unanswered prayers or we wonder what God has done for us lately. We forget the big picture as laid out in the Bible. We forget that we are called to engage with the mission of God. This wonderful God we worship created the beautiful world we live in, mourned when humans fell into sin, and sent Jesus Christ to be the redeemer of all the brokenness we can see so vividly and so painfully around us. The Sent One, Jesus, longs for us to understand that we have been sent into the world as he was (John 17:18), to act and speak in ways that reflect the love of God in every setting of life. When we live as if we have been sent into the world as Jesus was, we are participating in God's mission.

What Is God Up To?

Emphasizing our call to embrace the mission of God is often described as being "missional." A growing cluster of books and articles discusses this missional approach to congregational life and ministry, and throughout this book the word "missional" will be used to refer to an emphasis on engaging with the mission of God. Spiritual practices, individual and communal, help us embrace this mission of God because they enable us to hear and follow God's priorities. They open us to the voice of the Holy Spirit illuminating the truths in the Bible and guiding us specifically. They help us become more like Jesus, full of grace and truth. They help us to be available to God, whatever that looks like in our setting. Alan Roxburgh, in his book *Missional Mapmaking*, argues that one significant task of Christian leaders is to shape the culture in congregations and thus influence the wider culture. In the same way that the culture of a country has characteristics and trends, so also a congregation has a culture, the shared values and beliefs that shape that congregation's actions and social behaviors. Roxburgh notes that spiritual disciplines go a long way toward influencing the culture of a congregation. He argues that through spiritual practices,

> We are being reshaped in the imagination that our lives are gifts from and belong to God. We come to experience in a new way that none of us are self-made; we receive our life every day from God as a gift. Imagine what this new kind of character would do as witness to and transformation of our culture, with its focus on the individual as self-made. Imagine what might happen in our neighborhoods and communities when the people of a local church live for the others in their lives rather than for themselves.[4]

Radically different habits, he believes, result in a different imagination that shapes our understanding of grace and gift, and helps us understand that we do not make our lives happen on our own. He continues, "Life is a gift to be embraced, a vocation to be lived in the presence of God and others."[5] The key questions of the missional church are, "What is God up to?" and "How can we join in?"[6] These questions require the very skills that are nurtured through spiritual disciplines, the ability to hear God and perceive how to respond. These questions also require the posture that is nurtured through spiritual practices, a posture of receptivity and willingness to follow. As Roxburgh has described, our lives are gifts that have been given to us by God. We belong to God and were created to walk in Jesus' path communally, not alone. Resisting consumerism can make space for more of God's voice in our lives. And as we learn to listen to God for guidance in many diverse areas, we will receive the wisdom we need in order to live wisely in our materialistic culture. The spiritual disciplines discussed in this book can help us profoundly as we attempt to do these things as communities of faith. We are called not only to resist materialism and the values of the secular culture, but also to lean into the mission of God, to walk in the love revealed by Jesus Christ, and, through the power of the Holy Spirit, to show that love in our families, workplaces, and communities. Spiritual practices play a role in enabling us to do that.

Encouraging Spiritual Practices in Small Groups and Congregations

As I wrote this book, I collected stories from many people who have engaged in spiritual disciplines in their small groups or congregations. The chapters that follow will give many specific illustrations of what it looks like to lead groups of people into an experience of thankfulness, fasting, contemplative prayer, contemplative approaches to Scripture, hospitality, and Sabbath keeping. An appendix at the end of the book lists concrete ways that worship services, sermons, small groups, church newsletters, and Web sites can promote the notion of engaging in spiritual disciplines as a community.

Lent and Advent are wonderful times to introduce new spiritual practices or help people engage more deeply in the practices that are already a part of their lives. One congregation used postcards and printed paintings of the Annunciation, Jesus' birth, the adoration of the Magi and the flight into Egypt, one for each week of Advent. They put reflection questions on the back of the postcards, and encouraged members to spend time each day pondering the paintings and allowing God to speak to them in new

> *How we spend our days is, of course, how we spend our lives.*
>
> —Annie Dillard,
> *The Writing Life*

ways. For many in the congregation, looking at art in a meditative way was something new, but they were already motivated to do something different in Advent in order to keep Jesus at the center of the season. Many families already use Advent wreaths. Consider encouraging families and small groups in your congregation to add further practices to the lighting of the Advent wreath—perhaps prayers of thankfulness for the week or a breath prayer or the prayer of *examen* (see chapter 4). Consider ways the Advent wreath lighting in Sunday worship could be deepened and enriched with new practices.

Lent is another season of the church year when new spiritual disciplines, or the deepening of familiar ones, work well. One congregation suggested that its small groups explore Sabbath keeping during Lent by using a particular Bible study guide. Fasting has been a traditional way to focus on Jesus' journey to the cross in Lent, and congregations can invite members to fast in a variety of ways during Lent. Any of the spiritual disciplines described in this book would make an appropriate focus for Advent and Lent—times of year when people are perhaps more open than usual to guidance about how to keep God as a central focus for the season.

I am hoping that as you read this book, your thoughts as you read and reflect, and the practical plans that result from your pondering, will bear good fruit in the groups you belong to. May this book help you consider ways in which you might introduce new spiritual practices in your small group and congregation. May it give you language to help congregation members identify and celebrate the spiritual disciplines that they already engage in. May this book, and the reflection you engage in as you read it, bring an increased attitude of receptivity to all God is doing, and may your groups and congregations grow in experiencing the immensity of love that God poured out through Jesus Christ and made real through the Holy Spirit.

Questions for Reflection,
Discussion, or Journaling

1. When you think of the word "discipline," what comes to mind first of all? In what ways can you see the concept of discipline as a positive corrective to some of the forces at work in our culture today?
2. If a spiritual discipline is a practice, relationship, or experience that helps you keep company with Jesus and that trains you in faithfulness, what spiritual disciplines do you engage in already? In what ways have they shaped you? In what ways would you like them to shape you further?
3. When you think of your congregation being sent into the world as Jesus was sent, what emotions do you feel? What are you grateful for? What challenges do you experience?
4. Which individual spiritual disciplines are encouraged by the leaders of your congregation? Which spiritual disciplines does your congregation engage in communally? What have been the benefits? What further benefits would you like to see?
5. If you could pray one thing for your congregation, what would it be? Can you see spiritual practices playing any part in the answer to that prayer?

For Further Reading

Butler Bass, Diana. *The Practicing Congregation: Imagining a New Old Church*. Bethesda, MD: The Alban Institute, 2005. In this encouraging book, Butler Bass describes practices she has observed in mainline congregations that are thriving.

Butler Bass, Diana. *Christianity for the Rest of Us: How the Neighborhood Church is Transforming the Faith*. San Francisco: HarperOne, 2007. Another heartening book detailing Butler Bass's research on thriving mainline congregations, with further description of the pattern of congregational life and the practices congregations engage in.

Foster, Richard J. *Celebration of Discipline: The Path to Spiritual Growth.* 3rd ed. San Francisco: Harper San Francisco, 1988. When I have interviewed people about spiritual disciplines, more of them mention this book than any other. They say it is both helpful and challenging. I find it to be deep and rich.

2

THANKFULNESS

Let the peace of Christ rule in your hearts, to which indeed you were called in the one body. And be thankful. Let the word of Christ dwell in you richly; teach and admonish one another in all wisdom; and with gratitude in your hearts sing psalms, hymns, and spiritual songs to God. And whatever you do, in word or deed, do everything in the name of the Lord Jesus, giving thanks to God the Father through him.

—Colossians 3:15–17

Almost twenty years ago my husband and I began a habit that has changed the way we pray individually and in groups. At that turning-point moment, we decided to try to begin every prayer time with a few prayers of thankfulness.

At that time, my husband and I usually prayed together before bedtime a couple of times each week, and we had begun to notice that our prayers seemed repetitive, boring, and often desperate. We actually felt more beaten down after we prayed than before, because our prayers basically consisted of a list of needs, and describing those needs in prayer brought them to our mind in a discouraging fashion. Nothing in our lives seemed to be changing because we had prayed.

It was a stressful time. My husband was deeply unhappy at his work. Our kids had entered adolescence, and we were baffled and frustrated by their increasingly challenging behavior. I had finished a seminary degree and was a candidate for ordination as a Presbyterian minister, but I had no idea when or if I would ever be ordained, or even if I really wanted to be. I felt called to congregational ministry, but I was doing some part-time writing and editing for the presbytery and Synod, and writing was becoming an increasingly significant part of my life. I was worried about my future. Would it include church ministry or writing? How would I decide?

Dave and I began our thankfulness experiment. We lay in bed, tired from yet one more tumultuous day, trying to think of something for which we could express thanks. Our prayers of thanks were quite tentative at first. Some nights all we could manage was to thank God that we had food on the table and that the four of us were healthy.

A year went by, then another year. Our prayers of thankfulness blossomed even though my husband's work situation became worse, our teenagers baffled us more than ever, and I experienced no resolution of my job questions. We were amazed by how many things we could notice for which we wanted to thank God: friends, extended family, our neighborhood, bursting flowers in the spring, colorful leaves in the fall. We saw answers to prayer more readily. We were able to identify small miracles every day, like avoiding an accident in heavy traffic or remembering to pay a bill right before a late fee was applied.

The specifics of daily life became more visible to us as manifestations of God's care. We had always been thankful for food on the table each day, but now many more aspects of our life seemed to flow from the hands of a gracious and generous God: A warm home in winter, when homeless people shivered on the streets of Seattle, where we lived at the time. The cedar tree in front of our house, where squirrels scampered in the branches. Enough money to eat at a restaurant, buy a new set of dishes, or repair the damage caused by a slow leak in the bathroom. And we became more grateful for the specifics of the food we ate: the first strawberries of the summer, vine-ripened tomatoes in August, and warm soup on a cold day.

We became more aware of what we had been missing in all those years of prayer times that were packed with our needs and wants. We simply hadn't noticed God's good gifts to us.

Bless the LORD, O my soul, and do not forget all his benefits.

—Psalm 103:2

Looking back, we felt a bit ashamed of the "give me this, give me that" orientation of our prayers before we began our experiment.

I began to pray more thankfulness prayers as a part of my own personal prayers. And I began to experience frustration when I prayed with others. I was an elder in my congregation, so I attended session meetings every month and one or two committee meetings in between. At our church, all meetings included a time of conversational prayer, and I began to notice how quickly the committee members dived into making requests of God. I found myself increasingly angry and offended when the very first prayer began with a request.

I found myself thinking, This is the maker of the universe we are addressing! The giver of every good gift in our lives! And we have the audacity to come into the presence of this generous and gracious God without acknowledging our gratitude and our dependence? What kind of brats launch right into a list of requests? I got angry so many times in meetings that I finally began to take initiative. When the leader of the meeting would say, "Let's spend some time in prayer," I would immediately chime in and say, "Could we please begin with some prayers of thankfulness?" People were willing to try, but I was often frustrated that after only one or two thankfulness prayers, we fell back into our pattern of one request after another. Still, a few thankfulness prayers were better than none.

Several years after Dave's and my thankfulness experiment began, I was ordained as an associate pastor. (It was a half-time position, so I could keep writing, yet one more thing to be thankful for.) Now I was praying with groups of people several times a week. I always suggested that we begin times of prayer with thankfulness. The committees and other groups I was regularly involved with got used to my suggestion, and they grew in their ability to thank God.

The thankfulness prayers in my church groups sometimes focused on God's provision of money for a project or our gratitude for the volunteers who were making an event happen. Sometimes we thanked God for answers to requests we had prayed at earlier meetings. Other times we expressed our thanks for overseas workers connected to the congregation; for the health and safety of the youth group on their annual mission trip; or for the staff, elders, deacons, and other lay leaders at church. The possibilities for thanks were endless, and I began to see that others benefitted from my suggestion. All of us saw God's hand in our midst more clearly because we were setting aside time to notice.

I joined a support group of women clergy, and I made the same suggestion there. As a group, we grew in our ability to identify things to be thankful for. One of my most precious memories is a time in that group when we prayed prayers of thankfulness for forty-five minutes. One of the women was involved in a painful lawsuit, and we had been praying month after month for the seemingly endless developments related to the suit. In that day when we prayed a particularly long thankfulness prayer, we thanked God for situation after situation where something unexpectedly good had happened in the legal process or where God's care was evident.

In fact, for each member of the group, we focused on their areas of need, but instead of making requests about those needs, we focused on thanking God for the way God had already been working in those areas. So many answers to prayer, small miracles, and provisions from God were begging to be noticed, and on that day we took the time to notice them and to thank the Giver. I came away from that prayer time with a joyful heart at the amazing love and mercy of our wonderful God and with a recommitment to continue to pay attention to God's blessings in my life.

What We Miss

Prayers of thankfulness enable us to see what God has been doing and where God has been working. Prayers of thankfulness enable us to notice the specifics of God's work and the patterns of God's goodness in our lives and the lives of others. Prayers of thankfulness make us stop and look.

We are missing so much of God's work in the world because we don't notice. Advertisements bombard us with messages about what we don't have and we bring that spirit of lack into our prayers. It is right and good to ask God for what we need and for the needs of others, but sometimes I wonder if we are so influenced by ads that we bring an unbalanced perspective into our prayers. I wonder if we take a good thing—intercessory prayer— and overuse it to the extent that we are less able to pay attention to what God is already doing. The Jewish festivals throughout the year were designed to help the people remember the mighty deeds of God. For example, Passover harkens back to the exodus from Egypt, and when Jews eat the Passover meal they remember what God did. They remember it as they say the words of the Passover liturgy, and even the food at the meal represents the events they are remembering. We can't be sure exactly when people in Old Testament times prayed, but it appears that daily prayers were also designed to help people remember God's goodness by being connected with the recurring events of each day: rising, eating meals, and going to sleep. God is the one who gives the sunlight each morning so the day can start. God provides the food at mealtimes. God gives rest at the end of the day. These opportunities for thanks recur day after day. We retain something of this attitude of thankfulness when we say grace before meals, but we could use a lot more moments of stopping to thank God for the rhythms of daily life.

> *We aren't grateful because we are happy. We are happy because we are grateful.*
>
> — Douglas Wood,
> *The Secret of Saying Thanks*

This forgetfulness is not limited to us; it also afflicted the people of the Bible. Over and over, the prophets of the Old Testament tell God's people that they have forgotten what God has done, a problem the prophets identify as idolatry that comes from amnesia: God has done good things for the Israelites, but they simply don't remember, so they turn to other gods.

God created a beautiful world, and stopping to notice the beauty of flowers, mountains, sunsets, and even the fruits and vegetables we eat can help us thank God and remember God as the One who made it all. God is also our redeemer in Jesus Christ. God, through the Holy Spirit, gives us refuge from so many terrors and struggles in daily life. Prayers of thankfulness help us remember God's work of redemption, both in the past in Jesus and in the present through the Holy Spirit.

Isaiah, Jeremiah, and Hosea often speak about our need to remember God in these two roles of creator and redeemer. "You have forgotten the LORD, your Maker, / who stretched out the heavens / and laid the foundations of the earth" (Isa. 51:13), and "You have forgotten the God of your salvation, / and have not remembered the Rock of your refuge" (Isa. 17:10). Jeremiah describes the effect of amnesia: we get off track.

> But my people have forgotten me,
> they burn offerings to a delusion;
> they have stumbled in their ways,
> in the ancient roads,
> and have gone into bypaths,
> not the highway.
>
> Jeremiah 18:15

When we forget to notice the work of God, we get off the main road and straggle into side roads that don't lead us where we want to go. Jeremiah's vivid words about burning offerings to a delusion illuminate another aspect of amnesia. We forget God and what God has done, and we engage in the worship of delusions. These delusions might include our fantasies of winning the lottery, losing so much weight that we look like a model, or going on an all-expenses-paid vacation to Tahiti. The delusions start as a vague dream, but then end up taking up so much mental space that we forget to notice the work of God in our life.

Hosea sees a different kind of cause and effect related to amnesia. In his view, God gives us what we need, and because of our satisfaction, we forget God.

> It was I who fed you in the wilderness,
> in the land of drought.
> When I fed them, they were satisfied;
> they were satisfied, and their heart was proud;
> therefore they forgot me.
>
> Hosea 13:5–6

So many factors in our daily lives encourage the same kind of amnesia followed by idolatry that afflicted the people of Israel: the busyness of our schedules, the demands on our time, and the advertisements that encourage us to focus on items we could buy. God's goodness surrounds us—in fact every good gift in our life comes from God (Jas. 1:17)—but so often we simply don't see God's goodness and God's gifts because we are focused on what we don't have. Prayers of thankfulness help us remember our dependence on the God who supplies our needs. A few months ago I was telling some people about Dave's and my thankfulness prayers, and one person asked why we would narrow our focus onto thankfulness. After all, this man said, ACTS is often held up as a good model for prayer: Adoration (or praise), Confession, Thankfulness, and Supplication (or intercession). Wouldn't a focus just on thankfulness be as unbalanced as a focus only on supplication, or asking for the things we want? The man's question got me thinking.

I pondered the pattern of my experience in worship services, and I thought about my daily life during the week. In most Protestant worship services, our praise songs and hymns concentrate on adoration, so worship services seem to give us plenty of opportunity for praise. In addition, I often find myself humming a praise song or hymn during the week. My husband and I play CDs of praise songs and hymns when we do chores, and Christian radio stations offer praise music to listen to. Opportunities to praise God through music—to engage in prayers of adoration—are abundant if we choose to embrace them. So the first part of the ACTS prayer, adoration, is readily available in most congregations.

Jumping to the last component of the ACTS prayer, it appears to me that Christians usually have no trouble with

> *I will give thanks to the LORD*
> *with my whole heart,*
> *in the company of the upright,*
> *in the congregation.*
>
> —Psalm 111:1

supplication. When groups of Christians pray together, they seem to default into prayers of intercession, asking for their own needs and the needs of others. Prayers of confession, the second component of the ACTS prayer, may be an area where we could use some encouragement. Some worship services include prayers of confession, but many do not.

But when and where do we engage in thankfulness, besides saying grace at meal times? When do we take the time to look at our lives to try to discern the actions and gifts of God? When do we express our thanks for God's daily provision of food, a place to live, productive things to do at work or at home, and people who care for us and for whom we care? When do we look back over all the things we've prayed for, to try to find the places where God has answered those prayers? Jesus expressed frustration with the nine lepers who did not come back to thank him after he healed them (Luke 17:11–19). How is their lack of gratitude any different than ours when God answers a prayer and we don't take the time to give thanks?

Praise versus Thanks

When I was a young adult and a new Christian, I was taught that praise and thankfulness are distinct from one another. Praise, my mentors said, focuses on who God is, while thankfulness focuses on what God has done. As the years have passed and I have sung hundreds if not thousands of hymns and praise songs, I now realize that the distinction is not so clear.

If a prayer, praise song, or hymn calls God "Redeemer" and mentions the death and resurrection of Jesus, does that reflect who God is — the One who redeems — or does it reflect the work of redemption God has done in Jesus Christ? If it focuses on what God has done, should that be considered thankfulness rather than praise?

In fact, separating who God is from what God has done is almost impossible. This is visible throughout the Bible.

The psalms move seamlessly between statements about who God is and the marvelous things God has done. Many of the New Testament epistles do the same. We learn about who God is by observing what God has done and continues to do. In fact, in the Bible it's not just humans who conflate God's praiseworthy identity with God's concrete acts in history; God does it too (e.g., Psalm 136). I've decided that praise and thanks are two overlapping circles. In the place where the two circles overlap, we focus on the work of God in creation and redemption so that we can praise God as Creator and Redeemer. God our Creator made a beautiful world, and when we worship God, we often praise and thank God for that beautiful world. In the same way, we are invited to praise and thank God for the work of redemption accomplished in Jesus Christ and continued into our lives through the Holy Spirit. This kind of praise/thanks is an integral and valuable part of worship, both corporate and in individual daily life.

However, so often in our corporate worship and in our communal prayers we lack the opportunity to reflect on our lives in order to notice the hand of God in our specific workplace, neighborhood, home, family, and friendships. We miss the aspects of thankfulness that do not overlap with praise, where we take the time to notice what God has been doing today, yesterday, and this past week in our lives and in the lives of people we care about. We sing praise songs and hymns that encourage thankfulness, but we don't take the time before or after singing to reflect on our lives and list or recite the things for which we are thankful. Many praise songs and hymns — such as "Give Thanks with a Grateful Heart" and "Come, Ye Thankful People, Come" — exhort the singers to be

> *Thou hast given so much to me. Give one thing more — a grateful heart.*
>
> — George Herbert, *The Poetical Works of George Herbert*

thankful, but say only a little about what exactly we should be thankful for. Very few hymns and praise songs follow the pattern of "For the Beauty of the Earth," enabling us to give "grateful praise" to God for many specifics aspects of daily life: "hill and vale, and tree and flower, sun and moon, and stars of light," human love and relationships, the five senses, and even human thought.

Litanies of thanks are often used at Thanksgiving and occasionally at other times. Those litanies resemble "For the Beauty of the Earth" in listing many aspects of daily life for which we can express thanks: family, friends, food, shelter, work, service, and other blessings. A litany of thanks usually involves a statement for the worship leader to say, followed by a statement by the congregation. Another option involves two sides of the congregation saying the two parts, or men and women dividing up the lines. A simple litany of thanks can be adapted from Psalm 136 (verses 1, 2, 4 and 25):

Leader: O give thanks to the Lord, for he is good

Congregation: For his steadfast love endures forever.

Leader: O give thanks to the God of gods

Congregation: For his steadfast love endures forever.

Leader: Who alone does great wonders

Congregation: For his steadfast love endures forever.

Leader: Who gives food to all flesh

Congregation: For his steadfast love endures forever.

Using Psalm 136 as a litany can be overly repetitive because the second half of each verse stays the same for the twenty-six verses of the psalm. Many other litanies of thanks vary the language more significantly. Most prayer books include options for litanies of thankfulness, and a Google search will reveal others. With my passion for thankfulness prayers, I'd like to see congregations use litanies of thankfulness more frequently, simply because they list so many areas of daily life for which we could give thanks. Whenever I participate in a litany of thanks, I am challenged to thank God for aspects of my life that I have forgotten to notice. My thankfulness prayers are stretched by litanies.

The Specifics of Thankfulness

Any list of aspects of daily human life—such as the words to "For the Beauty of the Earth" or a thankfulness litany—can provide ideas for thankfulness. We need reminders of all the areas of life that reveal God's goodness. We often, however, need something even more specific than that. We need to look back at our own lives and try to see the hand of God and the goodness of God in the events and people around us.

In many ways, small groups are the perfect place to engage in prayers of thankfulness that focus on the specifics of life. In my husband's men's Bible study group, one man keeps a list of all the prayer requests. At each weekly meeting, he brings out the list and asks people to report on any answers to prayer. Then, in their prayer time, they thank God for those answers.

> *The world will never starve for want of wonders, but only for want of wonder.*
>
> —G. K. Chesterton, quoted in Warren W. Wiersbe's *Preaching and Teaching with Imagination*

Even without a list, people in small groups often know each other well enough to be able to point out where God has been working in another person's life. Sometimes we can't see the hand of God in our own lives and we need the perception and insight of others. Spending time discussing the way we see God's presence in others' lives is one of the great gifts of small groups. Taking time to express thanks to God makes the experience richer and deeper.

Even in groups that don't know each other as well as a long-term small group, we can provide options for a brief look back to try to discern the generosity of God. Sometimes when I lead a class or committee meeting, I'll ask people to open by sharing their name and something they're grateful for that happened that day or that week. Participants might mention the flowering trees of spring, an act of love by a friend, or a successfully finished task at work. Listening to all the things the people mention stimulates me to see those same kinds of things in my own life. Sometimes when I lead group prayer times, I'll leave a time of silence and ask people to name out loud or in their hearts someone or something they're thankful for, just one word or one name.

A focus on the specific acts of God is possible in whole congregations as well. Sometimes when I lead a worship service, early in the service I'll ask people to stand and greet one another and say one thing they're thankful for from the previous week. Or when I am leading a congregational prayer time, I will go through a list of aspects of life, giving about thirty seconds after each aspect for people to name, aloud or silently, something or someone they're grateful for. I will open the prayer time with a general prayer of thanks, then say something like, "Brothers and sisters, I invite you to name out loud or silently, a family member or friend you were particularly grateful for this week."

After a period of silence, I might say, "I invite you to name someone in your neighborhood or workplace that you are thankful for." I might go on to ask worshipers to think about something in God's creation that they are grateful for, then something good that happened in their community or workplace, then perhaps an answer to prayer that they or someone they love experienced.

In the congregation I attend now, congregation members sign up on a roster to take their turn to provide the "prayer for others," a prayer every Sunday focused on the needs of congregation members, the nation, and the world. One time, when it was my turn to lead the prayer, I told the congregation in a few sentences about Dave's and my experiment in thankfulness, and then I prayed the entire prayer as a thankfulness prayer. I expressed thanks for the medical care that sick people in the congregation were receiving and the ways God was comforting them. I gave thanks for God's guidance in local and national politics, for the many Christians who serve with relief and development agencies around the world, for the missionaries connected with our congregation, and for those who work for peace internationally. More than for any other public prayer I've led, I received many comments saying the prayer was a breath of fresh air.

In one congregation in my city, prayers of thankfulness are often expressed in a participatory style. The congregation meets in a school auditorium with a stage. Every Sunday a large tray with dozens of votive candles is placed on the lip of the stage within easy reach of people standing below the stage. A large candle, called the Christ candle, sits beside the tray. At the beginning of the worship service, someone lights the Christ candle.

At some point during the praise singing, worshipers are invited to come up front to light a votive candle. Each person uses a taper candle, lying on the tray, to bring the flame from the Christ candle to one of the votive candles. The congregation is instructed that lighting a candle represents our prayers to God. Each Sunday suggestions are given for the focus of the candle-lighting prayer, and many Sundays worshipers are invited to think of something they are thankful for as they light a candle.[1]

Testimonies

The specifics of thankfulness for God's work in our lives are often made most clear in stories. At the second church in Seattle where I served in a pastoral role (a very small role because I was also a PhD student), the worship service ended every week with "What my faith means to me." This was a brief time, right before the closing hymn, where someone in the congregation could come up front and tell a story about where God had been at work in his or her life. I have always been leery of an open microphone in a worship service, worrying that people will tell long-winded stories. However, this congregation had a great pattern for these brief testimonies at the end of the service. People spoke for two or three minutes, focusing on one event where they had experienced God's guidance or care. The stories were sometimes very moving, and sometimes more ordinary, but they reminded us all that we needed to be watching for God's presence in daily life.

The person leading the worship service would announce the invitation to come and share a story, and then wait. Sometimes it took a minute or two for someone to come forward. When I took a turn leading the service, I found it challenging to know how long to wait for someone to come up.

Another model that allows expressions of thanks from congregation members is the open microphone option that we just discussed. For example, a small urban congregation offers an opportunity for anyone to say something after the sermon. The Sunday I visited this congregation, about ten people stood up in their pews and the worship leader brought them a roving microphone. Several people made brief comments about what the sermon meant to them. One woman expressed thanks for an offering that was taken the week earlier for an overseas project. Another woman described what she called an "everyday miracle": a medical procedure that week had improved her vision, and she wanted to thank God for this wonderful gift. Someone else got up to thank the volunteers who had helped decorate for a special event. Many congregations allow an open microphone for announcements, which affirms that the congregational life is rich, robust, and not necessarily controlled by the church leadership. All of that is good, but this open microphone after the sermon allows for a different and even better kind of congregational participation. Responses about the sermon and expressions of thanks to people and to God nurture a lovely spirit in worship.

You were made and set here to give voice to this: your own astonishment.

—Annie Dillard,
The Writing Life

Personal stories in public worship can be more closely scripted as well. I have seen numerous times where the person leading worship or the preacher planned ahead with someone to come up front to tell a story. We are used to seeing this with missionaries and people going on mission trips. Others often have moving stories to tell, and hearing a first-person story as a part of a sermon or at another time in a worship service can have a strong punch. For people who are not secure with public speaking, or when staying on time is an issue, an interview format can work well.

One large congregation uses its annual meeting as a place for storytelling. Adding some stories about God's work in the lives of individuals over the previous year (all of them scripted ahead of time) has reduced the focus on money and details that used to dominate the annual meeting. The meeting has become a time of celebration of God's goodness in that particular place among those people.

Some churches use their Web sites or monthly newsletters as vehicles for personal stories about God's action in people's lives. Such stories help remind the listeners to be watching for God's action in daily life. Stories help us engage in prayers of thankfulness.

Thankfulness as Dependence

David Steindl-Rast, in his beautiful book *Gratefulness, the Heart of Prayer*, points out that everything is a gift, yet we find it hard to acknowledge gifts because we don't like to admit our dependence. In an era when independence, pride, and competence are touted as supreme values, and when we find it easy to believe we have earned everything we have, is it any accident that opportunities to thank God for all the specifics of our lives are few and far between? Yes, we can praise and thank God for salvation in Jesus Christ, a worthy and life-giving thing to do, but when it comes to the small aspects of daily life, surely we don't have to thank God for those. Surely we have earned them by our labor, and surely we deserve them.

The practice of thankfulness for all the small—and large—aspects of daily life can play a part in helping small groups and congregations draw nearer to God in dependence and trust. Steindl-Rast writes, "When I acknowledge a gift received, I acknowledge a bond that binds me to the giver. . . . The one who says 'thank you' to another really says, 'We belong together.' Giver and thanksgiver belong together."[2]

Steindl-Rast wonders if our society suffers so much from alienation because we are reluctant to offer thanks. I agree with him. It seems clear that our friendships and family relationships suffer when we feel uneasy acknowledging bonds with other people, when we hold back from expressing gratitude. In addition, I wonder if the lack of vitality in so many congregations comes in part from the paucity of our thankfulness. If Steindl-Rast is right, and gratitude is a central way to express dependence on God and our desire to be together with God, then we may be missing a primary route to divine intimacy.

Congregations can easily provide opportunities for thankfulness. Members of small groups can choose to point out to each other the ways they see God at work in the other members of the group, so they can give thanks. In small and large gatherings, prayers of thankfulness can be expressed. Leaders can create opportunities to remember the blessings of the previous day or week through sharing questions, moments of silence, or candle lighting. Stories about God's work in individuals' lives can be told in worship services, in meetings and other gatherings, and in print and online. An intentional focus on thankfulness brings the fruit of great joy. The words written by Martin Rinkart in the early seventeenth century ring true today:

Now thank we all our God,
with heart and hands and voices,
who wondrous things has done,
in whom this world rejoices;
who from our mothers' arms
has blessed us on our way
with countless gifts of love,
and still is ours today.[3]

Questions for Reflection, Discussion, or Journaling

1. Think back on your childhood and early adult life. What patterns of thankfulness, or lack of thankfulness, were modeled by the people who were most important in your life? In what ways do they continue to influence you?

2. When and where in your life do you give thanks to God easily or frequently? In what ways do other people help you experience or express thankfulness?

3. Colossians 3:12–17 lays out patterns for communal life. Note the encouragement to thankfulness and the connections between thankfulness and other behaviors. In what ways do you react personally to these verses?

4. Psalm 106 attributes the disobedience of Israel to amnesia, noting that the people of Israel forgot what God had done in freeing them from slavery in Egypt. Read the psalm and look for any causes or consequences of forgetting. What are your personal reactions to this psalm?

5. In your small group or congregation, what might be some fairly easy ways to engage more frequently in thankfulness? What are the obstacles? What do you see as the primary benefits?

For Further Reading

Steindl-Rast, David. *Gratefulness, the Heart of Prayer: An Approach to Life in its Fullness*. New York: Paulist Press, 1984. The title and subtitle express Steindl-Rast's main themes well. He describes the role of thankfulness in building intimacy with God and in increasing a sense of wonder and joy.

3

FASTING

Yet even now, says the LORD,
return to me with all your heart,
with fasting, with weeping, and with mourning;
rend your hearts and not your clothing.
Return to the LORD, your God,
for he is gracious and merciful,
slow to anger, and abounding in steadfast love,
and relents from punishing.

—Joel 2:12–13

In the 1970s, when Richard Foster did the research for his chapter on fasting in *Celebration of Discipline*, he couldn't find a single book on Christian fasting written between 1871 and 1954. He asks, "What would account for this almost total disregard of a subject so frequently mentioned in Scripture and so ardently practiced by Christians throughout the centuries?"[1]

Foster describes fasting as an ancient and timeless spiritual discipline that has helped Christians through the ages live out their faithfulness to God. *Celebration of Discipline*, first published in 1978 and still a widely-read book, began the process of helping Christians in Western countries rediscover fasting. Many Christians have experimented with fasting because of reading *Celebration of Discipline*, and as a result many have adopted fasting as a weekly, monthly, or yearly practice.

As individuals have begun to see the benefits of fasting, they have encouraged small groups and even whole congregations to fast. As groups fast, individuals within those groups gain confidence and vision for fasting, and are more willing to try it on their own.

Carol, a Presbyterian minister who serves a small rural church, has introduced fasting both to her family and to her congregation. Several years ago, Carol's sister Susanna was diagnosed with a brain tumor. Carol's family is divided about many faith issues, but they all agreed that they wanted to pray for Susanna. Carol organized her family members so that someone was fasting and praying every day for her sister. Some of the family members fasted from food, others fasted from electronics, media or other pleasures, but all of them agreed to abstain from something for the purpose of prayer on their assigned day.

The cycle of fasting and prayer for Susanna went around several times—with family members doing their part on their scheduled day—before the third doctor diagnosed the problem as a rare kind of cyst, much more easily dealt with than a tumor. The unity that the family experienced through the fasting and prayer commitment impressed Carol, who brought this practice into her congregation. When a church member is ill, she asks people to sign up to pray and fast one day each week for the person who is sick.

In Carol's congregation, members are grateful to have something to do when people they love are ill. They have found that fasting from a component of daily life—food or something else—helps them remember to pray on their assigned day and to focus their prayers. Knowing that someone is fasting and praying every day is also immensely reassuring for the people who are ill.

What Is Christian Fasting?

Fasting in Carol's congregation involved prayer for people who are ill, so the connection with Christian priorities seems clear. However, people today fast for many diverse reasons unconnected to the Christian faith. A naturopathic doctor encourages a fast for cleansing the body, and people fast to lose weight. Most religions of the world emphasize fasting in some form. In the past few years, I've seen numerous articles about groups of people engaging in a technology fast for a day or a week. They turn off all their electronic devices for a period of time just to see what life is like without them.

What, then, makes a fast distinctively Christian? Let me propose a definition: Christian fasting is the voluntary denial of something for a specific time, for a spiritual purpose, by an individual, family, community, or nation.[2]

Part of the impact of fasting comes from doing something different than we would normally do. Fasting involves giving up something for a specific period of time, perhaps a day, a week, or forty days. This part of the definition of fasting applies to any fast for any motive. However, note that someone who never eats meat or refuses to have a cell phone is not fasting. Those are lifestyle choices, which can be viewed as spiritual disciplines of a different kind if they result in

> *Fasting is not meant to drag us down, but to still us. It is not meant to distract us from the really real, but rather to silence us so that we can hear things as they most truly are.*
>
> —Lauren Winner,
> *Mudhouse Sabbath*

growth in faith and enable the person to keep company with Jesus.

Christian fasting is different than other kinds of fasting because it has a spiritual goal. A Christian fast comes from the desire to draw near to the Triune God and embrace God's values revealed in Jesus Christ and made real to us through the power of the Holy Spirit. While fasting, we may be called to pray about the place in our life of the thing we are fasting from, and God may change our desires and give us insight into ways we can become more centered in Christ. Therefore a fast may have the unexpected result of addressing habits or addictions, and fasting from certain foods or from all food may result in weight loss. However, the primary purpose of Christian fasting is not to change habits, confront addictions, or lose weight. Nurturing that central relationship with God is the main point of Christian fasting.

In our time, in Western countries, Christians are fasting from all sorts of things in addition to food. The many options are a welcome development, because a good number of people should not fast from food. Anyone who has had an eating disorder should never fast from food in any form, because self-denial of food can result in a relapse of the eating disorder. People on certain medications need to eat regularly. Children should never stop eating, and many older people cannot skip meals.

But anyone can fast from television for a day or a week. Or news media. Or listening to music, using e-mail, checking Facebook, buying lattes, shopping, eating in restaurants, or going to movies. And most people who do not have a history of eating disorders, even those on medications that have to be taken with food, can fast from sugar, meat, or other specific foods. Some people find fasting from all food, and consuming only water or juice, to be deeply satisfying, but not everyone can engage in that form of fasting. However, anyone can fast from something, and a spirit of experimentation, while also relying on God's direction, can guide the specifics of fasting.

Fasting in the Bible

The Bible provides further guidance about the spiritual purpose that lies behind Christian fasting. The Bible has about two dozen stories of people who fasted, spread throughout the Old and New Testaments. Some fasted alone, some with others. Kings, queens, and ordinary people fasted. In the biblical stories, prayer usually accompanies fasting:

— *Forgiveness.* The Jewish Day of Atonement centered on asking God for forgiveness, and even today Jews fast on that day (Lev. 16:30). Scot McKnight points out that feeling deeply sad, either because of sin or because of mourning, seems to evoke a response in the form of fasting quite frequently in the Bible.[3] For example, David and his friends fasted when Saul and Jonathan were killed (2 Sam. 1:12). Even today, many people find it difficult to eat when they're feeling pain, sadness, or tension.

— *Intercessory prayer.* David fasted to plead with God for the life of his unborn son (2 Sam. 12:16). Esther and the Jews in Susa fasted when they heard about the decree to put them to death (Esth. 4:3) and again when Esther made the decision to go to the King (Esth. 4:16). Ezra and a group of people travelling with him from Persia to Judah fasted as they prayed for protection for the journey (Ezra 8:21, 23).

— *As part of prayer and worship in the early church.* In Acts 13:2–3, fasting appears to have been a normal part of prayer and worship, and God spoke to the gathered Christians in the midst of a fast, telling them to commission Barnabas and Paul for ministry to the Gentiles. In Acts 14:23, leaders of new churches were entrusted to the Lord through prayer and fasting.

— *To nurture intimacy with God.* Numerous passages in the Bible link fasting with intimacy with God, a heart relationship. The prophet Joel says, "Return to me with all your heart, with fasting, with weeping, and with mourning; rend your hearts and not your clothing" (Joel 2:12–13).

The prophet Isaiah adds an additional focus for fasting when he recounts an argument between the people and God. The people ask, "Why do we fast, but you do not see? Why do we humble ourselves, but you do not notice?" God's reply is stark: "Look, you serve your own interest on your fast day, and oppress your workers. Look, you fast only to quarrel and to fight and to strike with a wicked fist. Such fasting as you do today will not make your voice heard on high" (Isa. 58: 3, 4). Isaiah emphasizes a perspective that Jesus will develop further. Fasting does not honor God when it is coupled with selfishness, pride, or violence. Isaiah continues:

Is not this the fast that I choose:
　　to loose the bonds of injustice,
　　to undo the thongs of the yoke,
to let the oppressed go free,
　　and to break every yoke?
Is it not to share your bread with the hungry,
　　and to bring the homeless poor into your house;
when you see the naked, to cover them,
　　and not to hide yourself from your own kin?
Then your light shall break forth like the dawn,
　　and your healing shall spring up quickly.
　　　　　　　　　　　　　　　　　Isa. 58:6–8

Christian History

In the early church, for the first few centuries after Christ, Isaiah's version of fasting was quite common. Sometime around 128, Aristide, a journalist, explained to Emperor Hadrian the way Christians lived: "When someone is poor among them who has need of help, they fast for two or three days, and they have the custom of sending him the food which they had prepared for themselves."[4] Origen and Augustine were two early church leaders who promoted fasting as a way to share with the poor.

Numerous early church leaders recommended fasting for other purposes: to prepare for baptism and Easter and to cultivate purity of heart. After Christianity became the official religion of the Roman Empire, and persecution of Christians ceased, the church fathers promoted an additional reason for fasting. In a time without persecution, denying oneself food became a way of identifying with the sufferings of Christ. All of these purposes for fasting, common in the early church, can help to cultivate a relationship with the Triune God and embrace God's values.

> Some have exalted religious fasting beyond all Scripture and reason; and others have utterly disregarded it.
>
> —John Wesley, quoted in Arthur Wallis's *God's Chosen Fast*

While Jesus doesn't instruct his followers to fast, he seems to assume that fasting will be a normal part of the life of faith. His instructions for fasting begin with "when you fast" (Matt. 6:17), and fasting was quite common for the first 1,900 years of the Christian church. John Calvin, Martin Luther, John Wesley, and Jonathan Edwards encouraged and practiced fasting. George Washington wrote in his journal about participating in a day of fasting when the British Parliament ordered an embargo on the Port of Boston in 1774. John Adams and Abraham Lincoln called for national days of fasting and prayer in times of crisis.[5]

Why, then, did fasting fall out of favor in Western countries in the late nineteenth century and for most of the twentieth? The roots of the abandonment of fasting go back centuries.

Rejecting self-punishment and trying to earn God's approval. During the late medieval period, fasting often took on a flavor of self-punishment and distrust of all desires, and those emphases lingered long after the medieval period ended. Fasting during the late medieval period also had aspects of earning God's approval, trying to prove to God that the Christian was worthy and righteous. Even well after the Reformation, those emphases gave a meaning to fasting that ran counter to the Bible's teaching about grace and forgiveness in Jesus Christ. In the nineteenth century, Christians in Western countries saw that some of those unhealthy and unbiblical emphases continued to shape the practice of fasting, so they evidently came to believe that fasting couldn't function as a healthy spiritual discipline.

Consumerism and the emphasis on meeting all needs. It is no accident that fasting fell out of favor in the nineteenth and twentieth centuries, around the same time that advertisements for every conceivable item began to escalate. Advertisements have indoctrinated us to believe that we need to satisfy every desire right when it sweeps across our minds. *We might suffer harm if we don't meet our needs immediately! We might die of hunger!* This seems to have carried over into many areas beyond food. Many novels, movies, television shows, and other entertainment media encourage us to believe that if we don't satisfy our longings for sex, a flashy car, a latte every morning, a fashionable outfit in a catalog, or the latest hand-held electronic device, we will be depriving ourselves unnecessarily. Denying ourselves anything for any reason lost its attractiveness. In Western countries, we are beginning to rediscover the significance of self-restraint in many areas of life, and fasting can nurture the kind of self-discipline that accompanies Christian faith.

Recovery of an Ancient Practice

Richard Foster's book, *Celebration of Discipline*, and other voices from diverse theological perspectives have helped bring Christian fasting back from obscurity in Western countries. Mother Teresa, who became increasingly influential worldwide in her last decades of life, emphasized fasting from food and other pleasures as a way to save money to give to the poor, grow closer to God, and pray for social change. Many people experience solidarity with the poor as they fast, and they find that fasting helps them pray more frequently and more compassionately for people in various kinds of need. Bill Bright, the founder of Campus Crusade for Christ, also helped Christians rediscover fasting. In the 1990s, he encouraged Christians to fast and pray for world evangelization.

Fasting has come back into prominence for another reason as well. As more congregations are sponsoring mission trips to other countries, Christians from industrialized countries have had the opportunity to see fasting in churches that never abandoned this ancient spiritual discipline. In many parts of Asia, Africa, and South and Central America, Christians fast regularly as a part of congregational life, with weekly or monthly fast days and particular prayer requests highlighted by the congregation for each fast.

> *Giving, praying, and fasting are all part of Christian devotion. We have no more reason to exclude fasting from [Jesus'] teaching than we do giving or praying.*
>
> —Richard Foster,
> *Celebration of Discipline*

My husband participated in a church mission trip to Kenya a few years ago. On their first Sunday, the American group worshiped with a Kenyan congregation. My husband was bemused to find an announcement in the printed bulletin about the monthly congregational fast day. The date was given, along with a list of prayer requests for the fast day. In that congregation, as in many parts of Africa, some Christians fast by giving up all food while others fast by eating only vegetables and fruit. In much of Africa, Asia, and South and Central America, congregations fast frequently as a way to focus on intercessory prayer. They pray when they would have been eating, and their hunger pangs remind them of the prayer requests for the day.

In Matthew 6:16–18, Jesus talks about looking for reward from God when we fast, rather than praise from other people. In the past century, Christians in Western countries have generally interpreted these words to mean that we must fast in secret as individuals. Christians in some other parts of the world see these words as indicating that our motives matter, that we shouldn't fast for show, but with sincerity and humility. As a result of this different interpretation, fasting in many parts of the world has long been a significant part of the communal life of faith. People share prayer requests for fast days and talk about what they believe they hear God saying during fasts, asking for the insights and perceptions of others. They give and receive support during fasts. Because of increased exposure to the practices of Christians around the world, Christians in North America, Europe, Australia, and New Zealand are rediscovering the joy of fasting in community.

World Vision has done an excellent job helping Christians to rediscover fasting in community. Their Thirty (or Forty) Hour Famine is a program that has been used by many church youth groups, and some adult groups as well, to engage in fasting as a way to experience solidarity with the hungry around the world. The program provides options for activities that help groups engage with issues of poverty and injustice during the thirty or forty hours they are not eating or are eating less food.[6]

Eastern Orthodox Christians
and Purity of Heart

Another influence that has brought fasting back into favor is the increased interest, on the part of many Protestants and Roman Catholics, in the Eastern Orthodox tradition. Fasting in Eastern Orthodox churches involves eating no animal products or oil, so it is basically a vegan diet but without oil. They also abstain from alcohol. Eastern Orthodox Christians fast communally on many days during the church year, and they feast communally at the end of their fasts.

Jason spent the first three decades of his adult life in a Presbyterian congregation. In his late forties, he became involved in a Greek Orthodox congregation. For about a year he divided his time between the two congregations, and then became a member of the Greek Orthodox Church. Jason has participated in many of the fasts encouraged by his new faith tradition. He remarked that information about the fasts is everywhere: "The priest talks about it a lot, and we have lots of devotional materials, calendars, cookbooks, and other helps."

When I spoke with Jason, he had just begun the longest fast of the year, the Lenten fast. For the past few years, he has engaged in this seven-week fast during Lent. He reflected, "The most practical outcome of this long fast is how it focuses the mind on Easter. I can see it out there, glowing like a star. That never used to happen to me. Easter sneaked up on me every year. When fasting, Easter seems like an incredibly long time away. Though at my age I'm starting to appreciate anything that slows time down!"

Jason noted that taking away food really gets our attention. He experiences fasting as a real pain but also a blessing:

The thing I appreciate about the fast is the same thing I appreciate about being Orthodox in general.

Being a believer isn't something that just happens in your head. You do things. Like make the sign of the cross. It's a physical gesture that actually connects you with the cross. As a Protestant, I would have said the value in the sign was symbolic, that it's good because it reminds you of the cross, but the *real* thing is the thought you have about the Cross. So I never made the sign, because why bother? Just skip it and have the thought.

The fast is like that. It seems like through mental will power you could spend the weeks before Easter in a heightened state of prayer and awareness. But most of us wouldn't. Fasting puts a piece of discipline on eating, something we all do every day. It does its sacramental work because our bodies are holy and the things we do with them have spiritual significance. So for Lent I'm saying my prayers and fasting, but I don't feel as much need to explain it to myself or make it into a system. Just do it. In the Greek Orthodox tradition, there's just so much richness of things to do. There's a lot to think about and meditate on too. It's a very rich life.

Fasting for Orthodox Christians never had a component of self-punishment or self-justification. For them, fasting is connected to repentance as a way to restore spiritual health, and to the kind of purity humans experienced in the Garden of Eden. It prepares the believer to receive Holy Communion and baptism. Fasting is a liberating experience that reorients the human will and provides an

> *In a more tangible, visceral way than any other spiritual discipline, fasting reveals our excessive attachments and the assumptions that lie behind them.*
>
> — Marjorie J. Thompson,
> *Soul Feast*

opportunity to discipline all the body's appetites in a way that brings freedom and health. Eastern Orthodox Christians view all spiritual disciplines, including fasting, as gifts we give to God out of love.

This emphasis on reorientation of the human will and the discipline of the body's appetites stands in direct contrast to the consumerism and materialism so common today. Perhaps we have begun to see that this inordinate emphasis on consumption is doing us no good. Perhaps we have finally reached a turning point, understood by Orthodox Christians all along, where we understand that we must stop satisfying every desire and appetite. In a world where we are surrounded by excess all the time — too much food, too many possessions, too much technology, too many e-mails and cell phone messages, too much encouragement to satisfy every sexual whim, too many movies and TV shows to watch — many people are finding refreshment in taking a break from some aspects of daily life. Doing it with others makes the experience richer, deeper, and easier.

People who fast talk about the way fasting helps them re-center their lives on Jesus Christ and recommit themselves to God's values and priorities. They describe the way their prayers seem more focused, and God's voice seems clearer. They say that fasting clarifies their vision and enables them to see the various components of their lives more clearly: *This action or this frequent preoccupation draws me away from God. I need to reconsider its place in my life, while giving more energy and time to prayer, Bible study, service, or loving the people around me. I need to reconsider the way I act at work, with my children, in my marriage, or with my friends, so that I can reflect Jesus' priorities more clearly.* The purity of heart that Eastern Orthodox Christians affirm in fasting is expressed by many Christians who fast frequently.

This purity of heart and clearer vision about daily life helps people stand firm against materialism and consumerism, as well as many other forms of excess. The implications of daily choices become more obvious, and the unmistakable results of unfettered consumption show up in stark relief. Fasting is truly a gift for Christians who want to grow nearer to God in an affluent world.

Those of us who experienced childhood and young adulthood in Western countries in the middle years of the twentieth century, when fasting was not on the radar screen in most churches, may be surprised to learn that fasting was such a normal and accepted aspect of the Christian life for most of Christian history and that it is still valued by Christians in many parts of the world. According to the interviews I conducted about fasting, many American Christians fast but don't talk about it, so many more people fast than we may be aware of.

Communal Fasting

Slightly more than half of the fasting stories in the Bible involve groups of people fasting together. For example, when the Moabites and the Ammonites, two neighboring nations, came to fight the nation of Judah, "Jehoshaphat was afraid; he set himself to seek the LORD, and proclaimed a fast throughout all Judah. Judah assembled to seek help from the LORD; from all the towns of Judah they came to seek the LORD" (2 Chr. 20:3–4). In the book of Jonah the Ninevites fasted together to repent, and in Acts, we have two stories about Paul and Barnabas and local church leaders fasting and praying together (12:2–3, 14:23). Some people, like David and Daniel, fasted both alone and in community. Daniel fasted alone when he was seeking an answer from God about how long the exile would last, and he fasted with his friends when they decided together not to eat the rich food of the king's court.

Fasting in community has a long history, going back more than three thousand years. Fasting with a friend, a spouse, a small group, a class, a congregation, or a community of congregations gives a sense of richness and companionship to the fast, an experience of being a part of something bigger. Fasting is easier when we know that others are partnering with us at the same time. Fasting with others mutes some of the negative voices that we can hear inside us when we fast, because we can rest in the fact that others are moving ahead with confidence. People who fast together can also feast together afterward, making the experience rich and full.

The simplest way to fast with others is to do it with one or two partners or in a small group. Congregational leaders who want to begin an emphasis on fasting could start by encouraging members to fast in pairs, in groups of three or four, or in small groups. Congregational leaders can provide resources about fasting to the congregation's small groups, encouraging them to consider engaging together in this spiritual practice, particularly in times of heightened need.

The benefits begin long before the fast starts. The participants can map out prayer requests and discuss their plans for the fast, how long it will last, and what it will look like to feast afterwards. They can also discuss fears and concerns. Participants can fast from different things, and they can even fast at slightly different times.

Participants can plan for the ways they will support each other during the fast. Will there be daily phone calls or e-mails? Meetings to talk about how the fast is going? Will they pray or worship together? They can talk ahead of time about the ways they hope to grow in prayer, and they can agree to pray for each other as they seek to listen to God. As they fast and pray, they can check in with each other about the ways God is shaping their prayers in new directions through the guidance of the Holy Spirit.

The time after the fast also has significance. The group can debrief together shortly after the fast, and then again several weeks later. Most people find that they continue to process their experience for several weeks.

Prayer and Communal Fasting

Simon is a Presbyterian minister from Zambia. His congregation in Zambia fasted every new year in order to commit the year to the Lord and to pray for individual and communal guidance. "These were times of recommitment," Simon remembers:

> We chose a day where we were all encouraged to pray and fast. No one was forced to fast. Everyone was encouraged to participate if they could. We were very aware of issues of people's health. We had medical people in the congregation who talked to people about how to look after themselves before the fast, and they gave advice about breaking the fast with a small meal, not a big one. People with medical issues were encouraged to fast in other areas, perhaps to do away with a usual thing like watching TV. This helped them feel that they could be a part of what was going on.

In Simon's congregation, everyone would gather at the end of the fast day for a service of worship together. He believes the fast, and the service at the end of the day, brought oneness to the congregation. "During the sharing time at the service, people with medical problems talked about how they had fasted, which revealed their health issues, and we were able to pray for them."

Another experience of Simon's in Zambia illustrates the significance of communal fasting. Whenever a candidate for ordination approaches his ordination day, all the ministers of the presbytery go on a weekend retreat with that person. They engage in a partial fast, consuming only fruit and water. "It is a time of consecration to the Lord," Simon noted, "and a time of reflection for the ordinand, a way to prepare for the ordination and the ministry that follows after it."

Whether your congregation is fasting to support a new ordinand in ministry, dedicate the year to God, or intercede for the sick, having a common focus of prayer helps make a communal fast work well. When fasting with a friend or small group, brainstorming prayer topics ahead of time can be an integral part of the experience. When fasting with a congregation or a larger community, the leaders of the fast often lay out prayer requests so everyone can be praying for the same needs. This partnership in prayer can be one of the great blessings of fasting in community.

Many people who fast regularly report that their prayers change over the course of the fast. Anna, a church musician who fasts frequently both from food and from things other than food, notes that she always starts a fast with specific prayer requests in mind. As the fast progresses, and as she prays for those specific needs, new concerns come up and she begins to pray for them. Often she ends a fast praying for something entirely different from the concerns she had at the beginning. Other times, when the fast ends she finds she is praying in a different way for the same needs she started with. These changes in prayer come from listening to God as she prays and reads the Bible.

The support of a community can be very helpful over the course of a fast as the direction of prayer changes. Having a partner or small group means having someone to talk with about the way God is guiding the prayers during the fast. Afterward, as prayers continue, the guidance received from God during the fast can help direct the way the group prays.

Fasting promotes dialogue with God. We listen for God to speak to us even while we speak our concerns and requests to God. We are wise if we talk over with our Christian brothers and sisters what we believe we are hearing from God, checking to see if they have heard God speak in a similar way. "Test the spirits to see whether they are from God," the apostle John recommends (1 John 4:1). When we believe we have heard God speak, we need to examine what we have heard by comparing it to the truth in the Bible and by discussing it in community. Fasting with others gives us that opportunity.

Who Calls for a Fast? Options for Congregational Fasting

As with any other congregational activity, a communal fast can be initiated in numerous ways:

— The minister, ministry team, or board can encourage everyone in the congregation to consider engaging in a fast. Specific prayer requests can be given for the fast that relate to congregation-wide needs.
— Any smaller group within the congregation—a home group, the choir, the youth group, a men's or women's group—can plan a fast and invite the rest of the congregation to join in. In this case, the prayer requests might be more specifically related to the needs of individuals or to the group that initiates the fast.
— An individual within a congregation can seek other individuals who want to fast communally, and after that group has made a commitment to fast, they can invite the whole congregation to join in.

Whoever initiates a fast, non-food options for fasting must be given so people who shouldn't go without food can participate.

Patterns of prayer during a small group or congregation-wide fast can vary as well. Some options include:

— Prayer together at the beginning and end of the fast
— Prayer together every evening of the fast for a fast of a few days
— Prayer together once a week for a fast lasting a month to forty days, such as at Lent

— Prayer together over the phone in prayer partnerships
— Sharing prayer requests and insights electronically through e-mail or Facebook

The most effective fasting in a congregational setting involves a good deal of education ahead of time, more than for any other spiritual discipline. Many people in congregations have prayed before, read the Bible, or practiced some of the other disciplines we discuss in this book, but fasting may be an entirely new experience that sparks questions: What exactly is fasting? Why fast? What is the biblical basis for fasting? What are the benefits of fasting? How can fasting be done safely by people with various medical conditions?

This kind of information is vital. How can it be disseminated effectively?

Let's imagine that a particular congregation wants to encourage a day or week of fasting by all members. The minister lays the groundwork by preaching on fasting, and a few people who fast regularly give testimonies in worship. The congregational leaders want to give people the practical information they need about fasting, so they're considering how to make that information available.

The first and most obvious option is the church Web site. A statement on the home page could present the notion of a congregational fast, with a prominent link. That link could take the viewer to pages with basic information about fasting, some biblical background, and suggestions for ways of fasting today. Testimonies from people who have fasted, explaining the ways fasting helped them draw nearer to God, could be written specifically for the Web site or could be transcribed from oral testimonies given during the worship service. Prayer requests for the fast could be posted on the Web site.

Many, many resources on every topic imaginable are available online these days. One of the increasingly significant responsibilities of congregational leaders will be to find appropriate and helpful resources and provide those links to members of the congregation. Links to helpful articles about fasting should be included with information about fasting on the church's Web site.

A church's Web site is of little use if no one visits it, so encouraging visits to the Web site is essential. A description of the information about fasting on the Web site can be placed in the printed bulletin. A Twitter post (or "tweet") could give the link to the information about fasting on the church's Web site, and additional tweets could remind people of the date of the congregational fast as it approaches. Facebook posts by congregational leaders could provide links and dates as well. E-mails from within Facebook could be sent to the members of the congregation's Facebook page or group. E-mail reminders—sent from within Facebook and sent using traditional e-mail—could include the fast dates, the prayer requests, and a link to the information on the Web site. If the minister or other congregational leaders have a blog, a blog post about fasting can also provide links to the information on the Web site.

After the fast is over, a few testimonies about the benefits of the fast could be placed on the Web site. Again, links to those testimonies could be sent out using Twitter, Facebook status updates, Facebook messages, and e-mail. Links can also be listed in the printed Sunday bulletin.

Printing the information about fasting on paper may be necessary for people who are not online. The presence of the links to other online sources of information will be part of what motivates people to look at the church Web site rather than pick up a printed booklet. Information about prayer requests can be updated online much more quickly as well.

Congregation members need help understanding the significance of what they are encouraged to do in the life of faith. Nudging congregation members to adopt spiritual practices is a good thing. However, it is even better to provide help interpreting the significance of the things they do. Sermons, blog posts, and personal testimonies in worship services or posted on Web sites can be good avenues for helping people understand the significance of their practices before and after they occur. (See the appendix for further ideas about congregational communication.)

When a fast has been initiated by a small group or an individual, information about fasting should be made available in the form of a recommended book, an online link to information about fasting, or a meeting where questions about fasting can be answered. Fasting is unfamiliar enough for many people that some information always needs to be given.

> *It is written, "One does not live by bread alone, but by every word that comes from the mouth of God."*
>
> —Matthew 4:4

The Gift of Fasting

The significance of fasting lies in its ability to help us draw nearer to God and to an experience of purity of heart and freedom in Christ beyond our immediate desires. As so many aspects of daily life encourage us to engage in excess, God is calling the church to find ways to step aside from the values of our culture and draw near to God in devotion and service.

Fasting, both alone and in community, offers a way to make that step. Fasting clears our minds, opens our hearts, and enables us to see Jesus more vividly. God's voice and God's call are more understandable and unhindered. We pray in new ways and with renewed power. People who fast are aware that they have entered into a mystery, and they are grateful for it.

Questions for Reflection, Discussion, or Journaling

1. As you began to read this chapter, what feelings and thoughts about fasting did you have? Did your thoughts and feelings change in any way as you read the chapter?
2. Using the definition of fasting on page 45, have you ever fasted? What form did it take? What was the experience like? What did you learn from it?
3. If you engage in a communal fast, what benefits would you hope and pray for?
4. Spend some time pondering Joel 2:12–13. What would it look like for the groups of people you are involved with—your family members, your neighbors, your colleagues at work, your small group, or your congregation—to "return" to God in a way that involved fasting?
5. If a group of people you are involved with decided to engage in a communal fast, what would need to be emphasized in order to motivate people to participate? What forms of fasting and what kinds of prayer for the fast days should be encouraged? What kinds of communication would be necessary?

For Further Reading

Baab, Lynne M. *Fasting: Spiritual Freedom Beyond Our Appetites*. Downers Grove, IL: InterVarsity Press, 2006. This is my own book on fasting, which expands on the many ideas in this chapter.

Johnson, Jan. *Simplicity and Fasting*. Downers Grove, IL: InterVarsity Press, 2003. This Bible study guide for groups or individuals takes on the disciplines of simplicity and fasting, with helpful notes for the leader.

Rogers, Carole Garibaldi. *Fasting: Exploring a Great Spiritual Practice*. Notre Dame, IN: Sorin Books, 2004. The author is a Roman Catholic, and roughly half of the book focuses on Christian fasting. The remainder discusses fasting in other world religions.

Ryan, Thomas. *The Sacred Art of Fasting*. Woodstock, VT: SkyLight Paths Publishing, 2005. The author, a Catholic priest, discusses the Christian tradition of fasting in a clear and helpful way. About half of the book presents fasting in other religions.

4

⎯⎯⎯ ⚬〰⚬ ⎯⎯⎯

CONTEMPLATIVE
PRAYER

For thus said the Lord GOD, the Holy One of Israel:
In returning and rest you shall be saved;
in quietness and in trust shall be your strength.
— Isaiah 30:15

I have had three significant "aha" moments that have
shaped my understanding of contemplative prayer. The
first came more than twenty years ago, when a minister I
knew described what she did every Friday at lunch time.
She served a church with three other churches close by.
Because the four church traditions were quite different,
the four ministers agreed that the one thing they could
all do together was to pray or meditate silently. They
decided to meet every Friday at noon for an hour of silence
together. They invited the members of their churches to
join in, and every Friday a group of perhaps a dozen gathered in silence, rotating their location from one church to
the next. The minister to whom I was talking described the

gift that an hour of silence every week had been to her. I was incredulous. *You do WHAT? You get together with a group of people for an hour and you don't talk at all? Why would you bother to spend that hour of silence there in a church building with others? Why wouldn't you do it at home, alone?* I didn't voice any of those feelings, but I left that conversation perplexed that the experience was so helpful to her.

Soon afterwards, my own church began offering contemplative events, sometimes in a class setting on Sunday mornings and sometimes at quiet day retreats on Saturdays. I remembered that minister's enthusiasm, so I went along to try out silent prayer with others. I learned how to do centering prayer and the prayer of *examen* (both of which will be described in this chapter), as well as *lectio divina* (which will be described in the next chapter). I took to contemplative prayer like a duck to water. I realize others don't always have the same experience that I did, but for me, contemplative prayer was like coming home. In the midst of the verbally oriented faith that I experienced at church and in smaller gatherings, contemplative prayer gave a sense of God as big and wild and wonderful—the mystery beyond our comprehension—and yet also as our refuge and fortress, a source of peace, comfort, and security.

The experience of engaging in silent prayer in groups was rich and life-giving, much more powerful and deep than engaging in silent prayer alone. Having others in the same room made a significant difference in a way that didn't seem logical and that I couldn't explain. The richness of that shared silence paralleled what I had heard from that minister several years earlier.

I enjoyed the sense of personal peace that came from contemplative prayer for several years before I had my second "aha" moment. This second burst of insight came from an article in the journal *Weavings*. The author, Robert Mulholland, points out that the outcome of contemplative prayer is availability to God.[1] If contemplative prayer involves listening to God, Mulholland argues, then we will become more attuned to God's purposes and goals if we engage in contemplative prayer. If contemplative prayer includes offering ourselves to God, then the more we pray in this way, the more we will be able to participate in God's purposes and goals. In other words, we will become more available to God.

I had been enjoying contemplative prayer for the peace it gave me. My life in those years was tumultuous and stressful, as I explained in the chapter on thankfulness. I came to contemplative prayer and found relief from the turmoil and a glimpse of "the peace of God that surpasses all understanding" (Phil. 4:7). But until I read the article by Robert Mulholland, I hadn't realized that contemplative prayer was playing a role in tuning my heart to God's values and empowering me to serve God more fully. The more I reflected on my experience with contemplative prayer, I realized that along with the peace, I was indeed sensing God's guidance more clearly and growing in my ability to follow God's leading.

> *Let praise be heard.*
> *Let prayer be spoken.*
> *Let silence fall.*
> *Let God be God.*
>
> —Susan Durber, Westminster College worship liturgy, Cambridge, United Kingdom

Contemplative prayer, then, is not just a nice thing to do that helps us find relief from the pain of daily life. It does do that, but the peace God gives through contemplative prayer enables us to look beyond our own troubles and issues to the wider world that God loves so much. It is a peace that empowers us to long for what God cares about and to engage with God in loving the people in our hurting world.

My third "aha" moment came several years later, when I wrote an article for our church newsletter about contemplative prayer. After a Sunday morning contemplative prayer class, I asked some of the participants to hang around for a few minutes in order to tell me what they wanted me to write in the church newsletter about contemplative prayer. I thought they would talk about the intimacy they felt with God or the depth of their experience of Scripture, but many of them instead related the intimacy they felt with each other.

One person said, "I like that you have an affinity with people without talking. God is joining hearts together." Another said, "It's a time to be alone with God but without loneliness because there is intimacy with God and with others." One person referred to liking everyone in the group, "a liking that comes out of quiet." The person who mirrored my own experience the most said, "Being quiet with God enables us to be a group. It begins with our relationship with God and then we can share it with the people around us."

I had experienced that sense of intimacy from quiet prayer in groups, but I hadn't realized others were experiencing it as well. Was the intimacy caused by the rich silence we experienced together? Did it come from the sharing we usually did after the period of silence? Did it come from the fact that all of us were becoming more available to God and thus more attuned to each other? Did it come from the shared values that arise when people become more available to God? No one in the room that day knew exactly where the intimacy came from, but they knew they were experiencing it.

In the midst of the busy lives that so many people experience, contemplative prayer can seem alien and foreign, as if we are being invited to do something incomprehensible. Why would we want to do this strange thing? Why in the world would we gather with others to do it? And yet the longing for a few moments of quiet and peace flows strongly in many hearts. Engaging in silent prayer in the presence of others is deep and rich, building intimacy and a communal sense of drawing nearer to God together, making us more able to walk with Jesus and follow him. For most people, engaging in silent prayer with others is easier than doing it alone. All of these are reasons for small groups and congregations to experiment with some of the forms of prayer described in this chapter.

Breath Prayer

Because of its simplicity, breath prayer is a great way to start when introducing a group to contemplative prayer. I know a family that engages in breath prayer at the beginning of their Sabbath day, and if the parents forget to make time for it, the kids remind them. I've used breath prayer in many different small group settings and occasionally in worship services as well, and most people take to it easily.

One way to engage in breath prayer is to imagine breathing out all our concerns and worries into God's presence, while breathing in God's love and care. At the Areopagus in Athens, the Apostle Paul said about God, "In him we live and move and have our being" (Acts 17:28). If God's presence and love surround us, then it is not a stretch to imagine exhaling our troubles into God's presence and inhaling God's love and care with each breath.

When I engage in this kind of breath prayer, I focus on one concern or one person in need as I breathe out. As I feel the air leaving my lungs, I picture myself relinquishing that concern or person into God's care. Then I breathe in, imagining God's love filling the empty space where the concern or worry was located inside me.

Sometimes the concern is so great that I spend several breaths on the same issue or person, always relinquishing the concern into God's hands as I breathe out, and always imagining God's love coming into me as I breathe in. Sometimes I simply name all my family members as I engage in breath prayer, saying one name silently with each breath out, knowing that God is aware of that person's needs even more than I could be.

Another form of breath prayer uses the ancient prayer called the Jesus Prayer: "Lord Jesus Christ, Son of God, have mercy on me, a sinner." This prayer is based loosely on the story of the Pharisee and the tax collector in Luke 8:9–14 in which the tax collector says, "God, be merciful to me, a sinner" (v. 13). One phrase of the Jesus Prayer is prayed on each breath, with the breaths providing a rhythm for the prayer.

In groups, I have used a white board to list the favorite names for Jesus that the group members suggest, such as Prince of Peace, Bread of Life, Light of the World, and True Vine. I suggest to the group that they pick one of those names and adapt the Jesus Prayer to that name, along these lines:

Lord Jesus Christ, Prince of Peace, have mercy on me. I need your peace.
Lord Jesus Christ, Bread of life, have mercy on me, feed me.
Lord Jesus Christ, Light of the World, have mercy on me, shine your light in me.
Lord Jesus Christ, True Vine, have mercy on me, help me abide in you.

Then we spend some time as a group praying the new prayer silently in harmony with our breathing.

Breath prayer works well as a first stage of prayer for many other kinds of contemplative or intercessory group prayer. It provides a good introduction to guided meditations. So simple and nonthreatening, breath prayer helps people relax and feel competent about silent prayer when they might feel a bit unsure about engaging in quiet contemplative prayer in a group.

Breath prayer engages the physical body and helps us experience God's presence in our bodies and in the physical world, integrating the physical and spiritual parts of our lives. Focusing on our breath slows down our breathing, which has the effect of slowing down all bodily functions, a way to experience peace from the One who gives us breath and longs to give us peace.

Breath prayer also reminds us of the Holy Spirit, the breath of God in our lives. When leading breath prayer with a group, any of these connections can be highlighted for the group, helping them to deepen their experience.

Guided Meditations

Another easy way to introduce groups to quiet forms of prayer is through guided meditations, which direct the imaginations of the participants into a scene where they might encounter Jesus. Some guided meditations use specific passages from the Gospels, adapting them so the people in the group can imagine themselves as participants in the scene, encountering Jesus with the other people in the Gospel story. Other guided meditations encourage participants to imagine a favorite place in nature—perhaps a beach, a forest, or a mountain—and then encounter Jesus there.

> *In the silence and solitude we are able to slow down, quieten ourselves and hear those things we so often do not hear.*
>
> —Trevor Hudson, "Retreat"

Guided meditations work well in any size group, such as small groups in homes or larger groups in retreat settings. I have experienced several fairly brief guided meditations in various Sunday morning worship services.

The leader of a guided meditation typically begins with a prayer asking God to guide the imaginations of the people present. The leader may suggest that the group members relax their bodies, perhaps even guiding the group through a process that focuses on relaxing various body parts. The leader may suggest that everyone take a few deep breaths or engage in breath prayer.

The leader then slowly reads the text of the guided meditation, allowing periods of silence for the participants to imagine themselves in the setting. One of the biggest challenges in leading guided meditations is to allow enough, but not too much, silence. I once led a guided meditation at a retreat, and afterwards a woman told me it had gone a bit too fast for her. I was feeling terrible about this, when another woman told me it had lasted too long. Perhaps I struck a happy medium.

Personal experiences of guided meditations differ widely, which is one of the challenges of leading them. My husband has always had a hard time seeing himself in another setting, so he often feels let down by a guided meditation experience. Some words of grace from the leader may be helpful at the beginning or end, affirming that there will be a wide range of experiences.

Sharing after Quiet Prayer

In any contemplative prayer experience, a decision always needs to be made about whether a time of sharing, sometimes called testimony, will follow the silent prayer time. For some people, simply engaging in the silent prayer time is enough. For others, the experience is not complete without an opportunity to talk about what happened.

The question of whether to offer a time of sharing or testimony comes up with guided meditations, with the prayer of *examen* and centering prayer, and with *lectio divina* and Ignatian Gospel contemplation, which will be discussed in the next chapter. If a sharing time is offered, participation must be optional. Forcing everyone to share, perhaps by going around the room with the expectation that each person will talk, can feel invasive to the more reserved people or to those who have had an experience they want to ponder for a while before discussing.

If the contemplative experience has been offered in a small group setting, the sharing time can be described as optional and people can be encouraged to share if they want to. The leader needs to be sensitive to allow enough time but not so much time that people feel pressured to talk. If the contemplative experience has been offered in a larger group, such as at a retreat, the leader can suggest that the participants gather briefly in groups of three to five people to share about the experience if they want to. Sharing in pairs after quiet prayer in a retreat setting is not a good idea because it can put pressure on everyone to share. If a contemplative prayer experience has been a part of a worship service, some option for sifting through the experience should be offered. One option is to have people available to pray with individuals after the service. Another is to announce that ministers or members of the pastoral care team will be available during the week for conversations about the experience of silent prayer time.

Guidelines for sharing after contemplative prayer always need to include a few words about the kinds of comments that are appropriate after someone has shared. In so many Christian settings—ranging from committee meetings to Bible studies to classes on contemporary topics—we are encouraged to analyze and to discuss issues with each other. Part of the gift of contemplative prayer to groups of people is the opportunity to hear from each other about the way we experience God, without the need to respond analytically.

I find prayer exciting because I never know in advance how God is going to meet with me.

—Joyce Huggett,
Listening to God

One of the people in the group I interviewed about an experience in contemplative prayer said, "I like the openness. There's a lot of space. I get rebellious if someone tells me what to do or how to think. Here there's a lot of space to have an experience, good or bad. It's very graceful and compassionate." When we make a time for sharing after a quiet prayer experience, we need to be careful to express grace and compassion in a way that makes space for a variety of experiences, all of them valid.

Contemplative prayer enables us to hear from each other the ways we are experiencing God, and process what we have heard from God. The proper response is to listen and appreciate, not to comment analytically—and absolutely not to criticize. Hearing about the work of God in another person's life is a precious gift. Therefore, sharing after any form of contemplative prayer needs to be received gracefully and openly by the other participants, without any feedback, analysis, or criticism. These guidelines need to be stated clearly by the leader before the sharing starts.

The Prayer of *Examen*

Examen is another good place to start learning contemplative prayer. Described in detail in the *Spiritual Exercises* by Ignatius Loyola, written in the sixteenth century, the practice provides a structure for looking at our lives.[2] *Examen* (which means consideration or examining) is a gentle, unforced noticing, an opportunity to look back on the past day or week to discern where God was present. *Examen* often was, and still is, used in monasteries at the end of the day, as a way to review the day. In *examen*, we invite God to bring to mind the way God was present during the time period we are considering. Going systematically through the schedule of the day or week is generally not a good way to approach *examen*, although that may work for some people. Casting one's mind back in a more general way, asking for God to bring instances to mind, is more often recommended.

The form of *examen* I have experienced in groups has four stages or steps, and the leader can announce each stage with a brief description, providing a framework for silent prayer that is not as intimidating as a long stretch of silence. The four stages involve two words that sound similar but have quite different meanings: "consciousness" and "conscience." The first refers to our awareness of God, and the second evokes our inner sense of right and wrong.

1) *Examination of Consciousness.* The first stage of *examen* involves looking back for the places where God has been present. This stage focuses on our awareness, or consciousness, of God's actions and care in our daily life. Were there moments of delight, love, joy, guidance, or conviction that seem to have come from God? Did God seem particularly real at a certain time? Did God answer a prayer or give a gift? The leader gives a period of silence to look back for the consciousness of God's presence.

2) *Response to Examination of Consciousness.* In the second stage of *examen*, participants are invited to respond to the awareness of God's presence, perhaps with a word or prayer of thanks, or even with a smile in God's direction. The leader gives a brief period of silence for this response, shorter than for the first step.

3) *Examination of Conscience.* In the third stage of *examen*, "conscience" refers to that inner voice that prompts us to acknowledge our shortcomings. This stage provides the opportunity to explore where God was present but where we resisted that presence. Did God seem to guide us to do something that we neglected to do? Or did God seem to lead us to stop doing something, but we kept doing it? Was there a gift of love or affection or joy that God seemed to want to give us but that we turned away, grumpy or irritable? Did the day or week hold opportunities that we resisted embracing? The leader gives a period of silence for reflection on the ways our conscience is informing us that we resisted God. This time of silence should be longer, about the same amount of time as the first step.

4) *Response to Examination of Conscience.* In the fourth stage of *examen*, participants can respond to God with a brief

prayer acknowledging resistance. "Lord have mercy" may be the best response, or perhaps a longer prayer of honesty. Again, the leader provides space for a brief period of silence, similar to step 2, so participants can respond to God.

Examen works well in small groups, and can be followed by an optional sharing time. I have led *examen* for the whole congregation during Sunday morning worship, and I have usually followed it with a traditional prayer of confession. *Examen* lays an excellent foundation for a prayer of confession, because the dual foci of *examen* — consciousness of God and the messages from our conscience — help people think more clearly about what they need to confess to God as sin. The prayer of confession also gives people one option of a way to respond to what they experienced in *examen*.

> *Never be rash with your mouth, nor let your heart be quick to utter a word before God, for God is in heaven, and you upon earth; therefore let your words be few.*
>
> — Ecclesiastes 5:2

Examen gives the gift of reflection on our lives, making space to watch for the hand of God and providing a simple structure to make observation doable. *Examen* helps us pay attention to the patterns of our lives.

Distractions in Contemplative Prayer

Several metaphors involving water have been helpful to me as I have encountered the inevitable struggles with wandering thoughts during contemplative prayer. The wandering thoughts can include worries and preoccupations about my own life or the lives of people I love, projects I'm working on that I can't resist thinking about, noises or other distractions from the physical environment, or even analysis of the spiritual profundity of what I'm experiencing. These distracting thoughts are particularly common at the beginning of a quiet prayer time, but they can unfortunately be all too frequent throughout the period of silence.

One of the people who led many of my early contemplative prayer experiences talked about these wandering thoughts as boats on a river. We can watch the boats, she said, and notice they are there, but we need to avoid the temptation of getting onto the boat and rummaging around in the hold. When we find ourselves boarding the boat and unpacking its contents, we can imagine ourselves stepping back off the boat and letting it float down the river without us.

Later someone else told me about the metaphor of a leaf on a river. This leader suggested that when we notice we have left the topic of the prayer and our minds have begun down another path, we view the random thought as a leaf. We let it float lightly down the river.

> *We are addicted to fulfillment, to the eradication of all emptiness. . . . We fear what spaciousness will reveal to us.*
>
> —Gerald May,
> *The Awakened Heart*

Adele Ahlberg Calhoun suggests one more river metaphor to help with distracting thoughts. She suggests that we imagine God's river of life running through us. Deep down in the river, the water is calm and slow, but the surface is cluttered with turmoil and debris. We can imagine our distracting thoughts as a part of that debris and turmoil on the surface, and let that part of the river be carried away by the current. The goal of quiet prayer is to return to the depth of the river where the presence of Jesus imparts peace and calm.[3]

I like the river analogies. Jesus compares the Holy Spirit to living water (John 7:37–39), and in Revelation, the river of the water of life flows through the heavenly city (Revelation 22:1–2). In contemplative prayer I relinquish my worries, my tendency to analyze everything, my preoccupations about work and all my other concerns into the hands of the Holy Spirit, who will take those thoughts into the River of Life. My concerns float lightly on the river like leaves. With the help of the Holy Spirit, those preoccupations and worries are not heavy and leaden. Instead, they float away, as light as leaves, entrusted into God's loving care.

Calhoun suggests another metaphor to help with distracting thoughts. Imagine, she suggests, that you are visiting a friend who lives in a busy urban setting. The windows are open because it is a warm day, and you can hear the street noise and the voices of passersby. Sometimes you even hear sirens. But you love your friend and want to be attentive, so although you notice the sounds coming from outside the window, you don't let your mind engage with them. Over and over, you return your focus to your friend. In the same way, in silent prayer, over and over you return your focus to Christ with you.[4]

Calhoun's busy street metaphor is helpful in a slightly different way than the water metaphors because it emphasizes relationship. Jesus has invited us to be his friends (John 15:12–17), and when we spend time with any friend, we can find distractions to be troubling. But our love for our friend draws us back continually into conversation, caring, and listening. Our priority is our relationship with our friend, and in any form of prayer, our priority is our attention to God in Christ, through the power of the Holy Spirit.

When leading contemplative prayer experiences, describing one of these metaphors for the group can be helpful, particularly with longer prayer experiences such as centering prayer, described below. Most people experience a lot of guilt when learning to engage in contemplative prayer because they are ashamed of their wandering minds. Everyone's mind wanders in silent prayer, and the water and friend metaphors can help us return to an awareness of God's presence over and over as we pray.

Centering Prayer

Many people believe that contemplative prayer always involves a long period of silence, and they know their minds will wander and they might even fall asleep. Therefore they are less than enthusiastic about attempting to engage in contemplative prayer. I have described breath prayer, guided meditations, and *examen* because they are contemplative prayer patterns that do not involve long stretches of silence. They are guided, enabling people to engage in some silence and reflection without having to fear long stretches of silence. Breath prayer, guided meditations, and *examen* can be used in almost any setting, with groups of almost any size, and even in large worship services, because they are structured, offer specific guidance and often steps to follow, and are not too lengthy.

The two contemplative approaches to the Bible described in the next chapter resemble the prayer patterns already discussed in that they, too, can be experienced in a group of any size or in a worship service. All these forms of prayer, because they are structured, are fairly easy to teach to a group and to lead. They provide a variety of ways to introduce contemplative prayer to groups of people, giving an experience of the kinds of quiet reflection that bring great riches. All of them help participants grow in their ability to rest in God's presence, even when they are not in a group setting. All of them help participants gain confidence that they can indeed meet God in silence.

Centering prayer, in contrast to the other prayer forms in this chapter and the next, does involve a long period of silence. The leader may provide instruction at the beginning, but the instruction is typically followed by a period of at least twenty minutes of silence. This long stretch of silence makes centering prayer appropriate only for groups of people who have made a commitment to this practice or who are genuinely interested in experiencing this form of prayer. Participants need to know what they are getting into. A leader should not spring a twenty-minute period of centering prayer on a group without ownership by the participants.

Because centering prayer involves a long period of silence, different authors give a variety of descriptions of what should be done during that period. The centering prayer instructions by Thomas Keating have been used in most of the groups I have participated in, so I will rely on his pattern from the book *Open Mind, Open Heart*.[5]

Keating recommends beginning with prayer, asking for God's help to discern a sacred word that will be the center of the centering prayer time. The word might be a name for God or Jesus, or it might be a gift that God gives, such as peace, love, or joy. The leader may read a Scripture passage to provide a possible focus for the sacred word, or the leader may invite the group to engage in *lectio divina* before the centering prayer in order to provide a deeper foundation in God's Word.

Sitting comfortably with eyes closed for the twenty-minute (or longer) period, the sacred word becomes a symbol of our willingness to encounter God in this time of silence. The word should not be changed during the prayer time, because changing the word requires thought, and the purpose of the time is to be open to God in a way that is beyond thought or analysis. Any kind of analysis during the prayer time is detrimental, including analysis of what we're experiencing or evaluation of the quality of the prayer. The goal is to be open to God, not to think about what's happening to us.

> *You have made us for yourself, O Lord, and our hearts are restless until they rest in you.*
>
> —St. Augustine, *The Confessions*

Sitting comfortably during contemplative prayer does not mean being so comfortable that sleep becomes inevitable. Often holding the back straight, with both feet flat on the floor, helps keep us alert. If sleep does happen, return to the sacred word on waking if at all possible.

Distractions and wandering thoughts are even more unavoidable than sleeping. Numerous metaphors, described above, can help us avoid self-criticism for the distractions. Gently returning to the sacred word restores the prayer focus. "Gentle" is a key word for centering prayer. We return to the sacred word gently, we treat ourselves gently when we notice our wandering minds, and we maintain gentle expectations of our prayer time. Overly high expectations turn the focus onto ourselves and what we're doing, rather than focusing on God's goodness and the voice of the Holy Spirit to us.

Keating recommends spending two or three minutes, as the prayer ends, with eyes still closed, slowly returning to awareness of the present. The leader may, in those few minutes, recite the Lord's Prayer slowly, or read a Scripture passage that provided a focus at the beginning of the prayer time.

After centering prayer has concluded, the leader may welcome the sharing of any thoughts or reflections that group members want to contribute. As with all forms of contemplative prayer, comments by group members are not to be analyzed or criticized by other participants, but received as precious gifts and as opportunities to learn how God works in other people's lives.

Other Ways to Reflect and Pray Quietly

Numerous other forms of quiet prayer that enhance our ability to listen to God can be experienced in groups. Some groups journal together, perhaps writing out their prayers and what they believe God to be saying in response, or perhaps recording their thoughts about a Scripture verse or biblical theme. Congregations are increasingly building labyrinths on their grounds or making a labyrinth on a canvas, and small groups of people walk the labyrinth together, praying and listening to God as they walk a stylized representation of the Christian journey. Groups of Christians sometimes engage in storytelling as a way to reflect on the work of God in their lives and listen for the voice of God.

Other forms of worship, prayer, and reflection that could be considered to be contemplative prayer include Taizé singing, meditating on a piece of art, praying with icons, or praying with a rosary or prayer beads. All of these forms of prayer can be led and experienced in groups. Small and large groups are increasingly engaging in various forms of art together with a spiritual intent and focus, including painting, making collages, working with clay, and writing poetry. Many people find that using their hands to create art, in the company of others, feeds their soul in unexpected ways.

Various forms of liturgical prayer can also be considered as a form of contemplative prayer because they encourage quiet reflection and help us listen to God. "Fixed-hour prayer" refers to liturgical prayers—printed prayers that are read aloud by a leader, in unison or responsively—that are designed for certain times of day, most often morning, noon, and evening. Often referred to as the divine office or the liturgy of the hours, fixed-hour prayer, when used in groups, mirrors the long monastic tradition of praying at certain times of day using liturgical prayers.

In the medieval period, when monasteries developed specific prayers for certain times of day, they were continuing a tradition that began far back in Jewish history. The words of the psalmist, "Seven times a day I praise you" (Ps. 119:164), probably refer to fixed-hour prayers that occurred every day at certain times of day. After the Reformation, liturgies associated with specific times of day were largely abandoned by Protestant churches, except Anglicans and Episcopalians, but in recent years many Protestants have been rediscovering these beautiful prayers.

Fixed-hour prayers can be used for a whole congregation. Compline, a worship service designed for the end of the day, is increasingly common. In Seattle, the city where I spent most of my adult life, and in Dunedin, New Zealand, the city where I live now, I know of churches that offer beautiful and meditative compline services accompanied with rich music, and many young people attend. Prayers from morning prayer services can be used in any morning worship, and prayers from vesper services can be used in any worship setting in the evening.

Fixed-hour prayers are increasingly used in small groups. A men's group meets at 6 a.m. for Bible study, sharing, and prayer. Sometimes they begin their time together by reading a morning prayer liturgy. A church staff gathers for lunch once a week and begins their lunch with a noonday prayer of commitment called *sext*. When a small group gathers in the evening, they start with the liturgy of evening prayer or vespers. Or they may read the compline service together at the end of their meeting.

The more often a person or group prays these fixed-hour prayers, the more familiar the prayers become. The rich theology in the prayers sinks into the heart, and the familiar words allow space for reflection, personal prayer, and simple rest in God. As with all spiritual disciplines, once is not enough. The benefits from praying fixed-hour prayers come with time.

Praying Alone and Praying in Groups

Many people find that after they learn contemplative prayer in a group, they want to engage in quiet prayer on their own. That was true for me. I learned how to do breath prayer and *examen* in group settings. After a while, I found myself doing them on my own as well, and the experience alone was often quite good. In groups, I love the sharing afterwards because hearing how God speaks in other people's lives is so encouraging and challenging. In groups I benefit from the richness of the silence, and I am able to pray longer. The actual prayer time is better in groups, but often I also want to engage in those kinds of prayers when I'm alone.

I enjoy centering prayer in groups and find it fruitful and enriching. My mind wanders a lot during the twenty minutes, but I am usually able to return to the sacred word. Coming back, over and over, after experiencing my mind wandering away, gives me something very vivid and deep from God. On my own, I have never succeeded in engaging in centering prayer for longer than five minutes, so I have never been able to return to the sacred word enough times to give the kind of depth that I have experienced in groups.

I am embarrassed that I find it so difficult to engage in centering prayer when alone. However, my experience illustrates an important point related to these contemplative prayer disciplines. They arose in communities in earlier centuries, and over the years they have been practiced frequently in communities. In our individualistic culture, when we learn about contemplative prayer, we think we should be able to do it alone just fine.

Engaging in contemplative prayer in groups does, in fact, help train us so that we can engage in it when alone. However, the main goal of contemplative prayer in a group is not to train us to do it alone. Instead, the goal is to grow in our ability to rest in God and hear God together. We can expect that God will speak to us about our own lives and priorities, but we can expect God to communicate with us about our communal life as well. The ability to hear God's voice is a skill urgently needed today.

Contemplative prayer enables us to keep company with Jesus in new ways. We open ourselves to be with Jesus as a friend and companion, and we welcome the voice of the

Holy Spirit as teacher and guide. In contemplative prayer we indicate our willingness, as individuals and as groups, to be shaped and transformed by God and to be available for God's purposes in the world. Contemplative prayer puts us in a receptive place that enables us to connect with other people in new ways as well.

Questions for Reflection, Discussion, or Journaling

1. Spend some time pondering the role of silence in your life. Is silence scary, peaceful, confining, liberating, resonant with love, or perhaps full of accusing voices? Does your experience of silence depend on your state of mind or the circumstances?

2. When you look back on your family of origin, what value or meaning was associated with silence? When you reflect on the churches you have been involved in, what value or meaning was associated with silence?

3. Have you ever experienced contemplative prayer in a group? What was the experience like for you? In what ways did it differ from silent prayer alone?

4. When you think of silent prayer in a group, what concerns come to mind? What do you think might be the benefits, or what benefits have you already experienced from silent prayer?

5. Look back over the kinds of contemplative prayer described in some detail in this chapter: breath prayer, *examen*, guided meditations, and centering prayer. Also consider the kinds of contemplative prayer mentioned at the end of the chapter: journaling, walking the labyrinth, and fixed-hour prayer. In what group settings can you imagine enjoying any or all of those kinds of prayer? What would it take to make it possible to engage in contemplative prayer in the groups to which you already belong?

For Further Reading

Johnson, Jan. *When the Soul Listens: Finding Rest and Direction in Contemplative Prayer.* Colorado Springs: NavPress, 1999. Johnson's style is practical and concrete with numerous examples.

Keating, Thomas. *Open Mind, Open Heart.* New York: Continuum, 2006. This twentieth anniversary edition of a classic book on centering prayer is written by one of the best-known authors on the subject.

Phyllis Tickle has compiled numerous books of fixed-hour prayers, most of them titled *The Divine Hours* and with various subtitles related to seasons of the year. The Presbyterian *Book of Common Worship* and the Episcopal *Book of Common Prayer* also have liturgies for morning and evening, as well as for other occasions.

5

⚮

CONTEMPLATIVE APPROACHES TO SCRIPTURE

Happy are those
who do not follow the advice of the wicked,
or take the path that sinners tread,
or sit in the seat of scoffers;
but their delight is in the law of the LORD,
and on his law they meditate day and night.
They are like trees
planted by streams of water,
which yield their fruit in its season,
and their leaves do not wither.
In all that they do, they prosper.
—Psalm 1:1–3

Janet and I meet at the front door of the church and walk inside together. We're on our way to the Sunday morning contemplative prayer class.

In the hall I notice her earrings—clear greenish-blue stones, big enough to sparkle and shine. I'm captured by the clarity of the stones, like water in a flowing mountain stream. "Those are great earrings," I say. "What kind of stone are they?"

"Aquamarine," she responds. "They were a gift when I was in my early twenties, and I've always loved them." I love them, too.

We enter into the prayer room and take adjoining seats. The leader hands us and the other dozen people a sheet with ten verses from John 6 on the top of the sheet, including verses 48 and 49: "I am the bread of life. Your ancestors ate the manna in the wilderness, and they died." At the bottom of the sheet are the words *lectio divina* followed by four steps with brief instructions after each step.

I've participated in *lectio divina* a few times before, but I can't remember the four steps very well, so I study the sheet as the leader introduces them briefly. She stresses that *lectio divina* isn't a rigid, cognitive process. Instead, she says, it's a way of sitting with a passage from the Bible and letting the Bible speak into our lives. She reminds us that the first step is to read the passage, watching for a word or phrase that jumps out at us. She says the word or phrase might "shimmer." She reads the passage aloud slowly and carefully, and then asks another participant to read the passage a second time. As she reads, the words "bread of life" pop out for me.

The leader strikes a resonant bell to mark the beginning of a ten-minute period of silence in which we are invited to work through the remaining three steps, with the shimmering word or phrase at the forefront of our minds. Janet is sitting next to me, and I notice again those beautiful earrings. The clarity of the stones is amazing. I'd really love to have those earrings. . . .

I return to the biblical passage printed on the sheet of paper. Yes, right, Jesus is the Bread of Life. I glance at the bottom of the page, where the four steps are listed.

The second step in *lectio divina* invites us to meditate on the word or phrase that jumped out, to ponder its meaning. Bread of Life. Food for the soul. Strength for the journey. Something that will nurture my inner life much more than those earrings would. But still, the beauty of those earrings reflects the Creator who made those amazing stones, so it can't be all bad to think about those earrings. I wonder if I could ask for earrings like that for Christmas. . . .

I return to the passage. Maybe it's time to move on to the third step, praying from the heart for something related to the word or phrase that shimmered. *Oh Lord, I really love jewelry, but I know this is a time where I'm supposed to focus on my love for you.* I sneak another glance at Janet's earrings. They are lovely.

I close my eyes again. You're the Bread of Life. Please feed me so I long for more of you, rather than more glittery toys. Please teach me what really matters in life. Be the Bread of Life for me in my daily life. Be the Bread of Life for me today.

The fourth step invites us to wait in silence for God to speak to us, perhaps in a metaphor or image. I force myself to close my eyes, straining to listen for something from God to penetrate my avaricious soul. In the silence, with my eyes firmly shut, I find myself struck by the soft texture, beautiful smell and delicious flavor of bread, in contrast to brittle hard stones—including aquamarines!—without scent or flavor. The vivid contrast makes me realize I want my own heart to be soft. I want to feed on the Bread of Life and let Jesus' loving character permeate my life. I want to convey the fragrance of Christ to people around me. I don't want to be obsessed with possessions, no matter how much they glitter, no matter if they are something beautiful created by God.

The leader rings the lovely bell again to indicate that our silent time has ended. She prays a brief prayer, thanking God for the Word that never stops speaking to us. She asks if anyone wants to talk about what he or she experienced.

The first person to speak mentions the wilderness experiences of her own life, and the way God met her there and fed her soul. I am astonished that I completely missed the reference to wilderness, a theme that often speaks powerfully to me. A second person says that "ancestors" shimmered for him, and talks about the people who shaped his faith and helped him draw near to Jesus as the Bread of Life. I am taken aback at the different experiences from the same passage. I was so absorbed with my own inner debate about stones and bread that I completely missed these other emphases.

As I leave the room, I am both amused and frustrated by my inability to maintain a consistent focus on the Scripture at hand. But I also know that God has met me through the words about Jesus, the Bread of Life. And those beautiful and distracting earrings actually played a role in the way God spoke to me. Truly the Holy Spirit does speak into my real life and my ridiculously obsessive thoughts when I open myself to the Word of God in a meditative and receptive posture.

Lectio Divina in Its Traditional Form

Lectio divina simply means "sacred reading." Meditation or contemplation on the Bible has been valued throughout Christian history, and *lectio divina* in various forms existed for more than a thousand years before being formalized into four movements in the twelfth century by Guido II, the ninth prior of the Grand Chartreuse in France. Guido was motivated to continue the long tradition of Bible meditation, while acknowledging the new reverence for reason that was coming to the forefront with the advent of scholasticism.

> Lectio *is listening to a Person present.*
>
> —Basil M. Pennington, *Lectio Divina*

Thus the movements of *lectio* have a structure and rational flavor, while facilitating spiritual engagement with the Scriptures.

I learned *lectio divina* in a contemplative prayer class in my church twenty years ago, and in the next few years I experienced it frequently in contemplative prayer classes and at prayer retreats. We engaged in *lectio* communally in a way that was quite faithful to Guido's intent. As I described above, we gathered in a group, and the leader passed out a handout. At the top of the handout was a passage from the Bible, usually ranging from five to fifteen verses long. At the bottom of the handout the four movements of *lectio divina* were listed with the Latin names that Guido gave them, followed by the meaning in English and a brief description of each movement, like this:

— *Lectio* (read). Read the passage slowly, watching for a word or phrase that jumps out or shines.
— *Meditatio* (meditate). Ponder the meaning of the word or phrase that struck you.
— *Oratio* (pray). Pray from the heart in response to the text any kind of prayer: adoration, thanksgiving, intercession, confession, lament, and so forth.
— *Contemplatio* (contemplate). Wait for God to speak to you, perhaps in an image or metaphor.

After passing out the handout, the leader gave a brief description of the four movements. He or she opened in prayer and then read the passage aloud once or twice, with the encouragement that we read it again, silently and slowly, as we entered into a time of silence. In the ten- to fifteen-minute period of silence during my own first attempts with *lectio divina*, we reflected on the passage, using the description of the four steps. In those early experiences, I worked my way systematically through the four steps in sequence, spending about a quarter of the time on each step and trying to engage strictly with the format.

Many times, my faithful, even rigid, engagement with the four movements created a fruitful experience for me. Those were priceless times of hearing God speak to me through the words of Scripture, so I became quite enthusiastic about the formal structure of *lectio*. I appreciated the way the four steps built on each other; I could simply observe and notice in the first step, then use my mind in the second step. Yet I didn't stay in a cognitive mode because those thoughts would be transformed into a response to God in the third step. I liked the way the waiting on God in the fourth step had a foundation to it; the waiting and listening was rooted in whatever I had received from the Scripture in steps 1 and 2, and also shaped by my prayers in step 3.

Several years later, I learned that the four movements could be done in a different order, that perhaps a person might be led to pray or rest in God right after the first movement. Several years after that, I learned that some people move through a passage, repeating the steps over and over, rather than spending a long time on each step. They might read the passage and watch for a word or phrase that sparkles, stop there, meditate, pray and contemplate that word or phrase, and then read on until another word or phrase calls out; they would then repeat the steps over and over, moving through the passage. And several years after that I heard about some of the ways leaders adapt the steps for group experiences of *lectio*, which I'll describe below.

> Lectio *is a disciplined form of devotion and not a method of Bible study. It is done purely and simply to come and to know God, to be brought before His Word, to listen.*
>
> —Gabriel O'Donnell, "Reading for Holiness" in *Spiritual Traditions for the Contemporary Church*

Guido described the four movements of *lectio divina* as four rungs on a ladder. While his intention was not to create a rigid system, and he encouraged some degree of flexibility in the way participants engage with the four movements, he also believed strongly in the close connections between the four movements, the kinds of connections I had experienced: "Reading without meditation is dry. Meditation without reading is subject to error. Prayer without meditation is lukewarm. Meditation without prayer is fruitless. Prayer with devotion leads to contemplation whereas contemplation without prayer happens rarely or by a miracle."[1]

Some Patterns of *Lectio Divina* for Groups

A couple of years ago, Elizabeth became the executive of a presbytery, a regional grouping of Presbyterian congregations. She was excited about her new role because this particular presbytery was in a time of deliberate change. The ministers and elders wanted to grow in their ability to make decisions by discernment rather than voting, and they wanted their relationships within the presbytery to become more collegial rather than management-focused.

As a part of this focus, Elizabeth began a presbytery-wide, monthly gathering for contemplative prayer and *lectio divina*. In each monthly session perhaps a dozen ministers, elders, and presbytery staff members gather and greet one another, then enter into a ten- or twenty-minute time of centering prayer (which is described in chapter 4). Then Elizabeth leads a corporate time of *lectio divina*. Elizabeth marks the four traditional movements of *lectio divina* by reading the Scripture aloud four times. She engages with the patterns of the four traditional movements, but she makes changes based on the specific passage chosen for the day.

Before reading the passage aloud for the first time, she asks participants to listen for something that jumps out at them and then to ponder those words in silence. After about two minutes, she reads the passage again, this time inviting them to see if something new strikes them or to imagine themselves in the scene. After this second two-minute period of silence, she reads the passage a third time, asking them to ponder a question related to the specific passage, either through journaling or silent reflection. This third period of silence lasts for a full twenty minutes to allow for deep contemplation. After this long silence, she reads the passage aloud for the fourth time, giving them another brief period of silence but this time with no particular instructions.

After the last brief period of silence, Elizabeth asks participants to share whatever they'd like to say. Over the two years of engagement in this communal practice, Elizabeth has observed that the nature of the sharing is different than the kind of conversation that happens in other settings. "In so many settings, we've gotten used to building surface relationships based on nonspiritual interactions," she explains. "Contemplating Scripture together, expecting that God will speak to each person, allows us to deepen relationships based on our engagement with Christ."

She believes that *lectio divina* removes the common pattern in Bible studies where the leader, and sometimes the participants as well, have an agenda or an axe to grind:

Bible study leaders or teachers have a perspective, a point of view. And the people in Bible studies have a variety of points of view as well, and they have ways of interpreting the Bible that are important to them. In Bible studies, participants often feel that they need to convince others of their perspective. In *lectio*, we each let God talk to us and we share what God has said, without trying to persuade the other people of anything. We're not here to criticize or evaluate other people's experience. In the sharing time, participants in *lectio* are free to ask questions or say how they view things, but not to debate. This gives us a place for spiritual conversations without an agenda, which enables us to grow in trusting one another's faith and love for God.

Elizabeth has a background in theater, and she believes the church today, in a time of such rapid change, needs improvisational skills. "A good improv team in a theater group knows each other well and tries to think ahead about what's coming. *Lectio* enables us to do that, to grow in trusting that others have a valid faith experience even when we might disagree with them on some particular issue. *Lectio* helps us be together in the Word, so we can be together in faith."

In addition, Elizabeth noted that *lectio divina* in a group enables participants to spend time with God outside the tasks and responsibilities of work, but to do it with others so that it becomes a counterpoint to the busyness and isolation that permeate so many lives. *Lectio divina* functions like a Sabbath moment for participants, quietly building community.

Other Communal Models

Because I spent so many years engaged with the four movements in a way that closely mirrors the intent of its inventor, I was quite surprised to learn about the ways that church leaders are adapting *lectio divina* for use in groups. Elizabeth leads *lectio* in the monthly gatherings in her presbytery in a four-step pattern, but the steps are not identical to those devised by Guido. Yet many of the components Guido advised are present in the way Elizabeth takes groups through four periods of meditation on a passage from the Bible.

> Lectio divina . . . *is a school in which we learn Christ.*
>
> —Michael Casey, *Sacred Reading*

Another minister, Jonathan, has led *lectio divina* communally in all three congregations where he has served. He has led it for youth, young adults, church leaders and church staff. He has led it for small and large groups. Jonathan, like Elizabeth, incorporates the four movements devised by Guido, but he has adapted them into a pattern that seems to work well in groups. Before beginning, Jonathan asks two different people to be prepared to read the passage aloud. He tries to be sure that both genders are represented. The *lectio* begins with the first volunteer reading the passage aloud. After the first reading, Jonathan invites people to pay attention to anything that stands out during the second reading. Nothing is forced; he just asks them to be open to a word, an idea, a question, a visual image or even a personal visceral response that "catches" them. He encourages participants, once they focus on something, not to worry about the rest of the passage, but instead to just go with whatever is grabbing them. If a Gospel or other narrative passage has been read, he often asks participants during the second reading to imagine the scene visually, opening up their other senses imaginatively and looking for what aspect of the scene tugs at them. After the two oral readings, he invites participants into a time of silence of two to three minutes focused on what stood out. Sometimes he picks a theme from the passage and asks participants to ponder that theme in the moments of silence.

After the time of silence, he asks people to talk about what they noticed or experienced. He encourages "I wonder . . ." questions. Then he usually passes out a piece of paper with the passage from the Bible printed on it. He suggests that people read the passage again, this time silently, followed by another period of silence. He invites participants to pray the text in whatever way feels appropriate to them, with particular emphasis on the moment or aspect that struck them in the passage. He asks them to give themselves to that moment, and then pray about it. They can write their prayer if they wish, or draw something, or simply pray silently. If they prefer, they can simply rest in that moment.

After the second period of silence, Jonathan again invites people to talk. Usually the conversation focuses on what stood out to people, or where they were "caught." At this time he sometimes follows up with a fairly focused sharing question based on the content of the passage. Like all sharing after a period of contemplative prayer, Jonathan invites people to describe their own experiences without evaluating the experience of others. Jonathan, like Elizabeth, notes that this practice helps people grow in their ability to trust the faith journeys of other people, because the sharing focuses on the ways God is speaking to each person.

Sometimes, to close the session, he reads the passage one last time and invites people to let the Scripture "wash over" them, or let the whole passage become a prayer in and of itself, with no other particular instruction or invitation. He then ends with a benediction.

Lectio Divina in a Variety of Settings

A contemplative prayer group, class, or retreat is a logical place for engagement in *lectio divina* because people are coming with the expectation that there will be silent reflection. Many other settings in congregational life can also be appropriate, even though they might seem at first glance to be less likely places for *lectio*. Four settings where people in your congregation may wish to try *lectio* include:

1) *Bible study groups and other small groups.* Rebecca, a minister, testified to the benefits of *lectio divina* in small groups, saying:

I was in a group that had a lot of knowledge—two people with a PhD, three people with an MDiv, four folks in full-time ministry—and we sometimes struggled a bit doing a Bible study together. Often it was too much in our heads or we disagreed on the approach. We were a group of eleven and one week it happened that only six of us were there. No one had prepared anything. So I suggested (a little meekly as this was 1999 and *lectio* was new on the scene for Protestants) trying *lectio divina*. We did it and everyone loved it. We introduced it to the rest of the group and continued with it until we stopped meeting about a year ago.

For a season, Rebecca's group adopted the practice of having an inductive Bible study one week, ranging from a few verses to a whole chapter, then a *lectio* experience in the following meeting on the same text. "It was great to watch as one session informed another," Rebecca remembered. "I think it was also powerful to hear the word or phrase that spoke to you uttered by another person as it spoke to them."

2) *Church boards*. Boards and committees might also seem like unlikely places for *lectio*. At the church where I learned *lectio divina*, session meetings always begin with a devotion by an elder, and some of those elders led the session in a *lectio divina* of a short passage from the Bible. The minister at that church, when he looked back at the pattern of devotions at session meetings during his time there, remembered those devotions involving *lectio* as being especially fruitful. He noted, "We feed each other better in community than by ourselves."

3) *Church staff gatherings*. Another example of the impact of communal *lectio divina* and contemplative prayer comes from Will, who began a contemplative prayer and *lectio divina* practice with his church staff, which continued after Will moved to another post. Three mornings a week, Tuesday through Thursday, Will invited staff members to gather at 8:30 a.m. for a communal time of prayer and reflection on the Bible that lasted for an hour. On

Wednesdays, the time focused on centering prayer and *examen*, followed by reading a book on prayer together. On Tuesdays and Thursdays, the staff members were encouraged to spend thirty minutes on their own engaged in *lectio divina*. Then they would gather to read the morning office, a liturgical worship service, together.

The influence on the staff was profound, Will believes. "These practices gave us the ability to be present to each other and to God, to be earthed in our own stories. We grew in our ability to be nonreactive, to acknowledge things that were troubling us and to identify our own thoughts, and then to release them. After some time, there was an impact on the wider church, beginning with the leadership community of the congregation. What we had learned radiated out from us."

4) *Worship services.* Several times a year, George leads his congregation in *lectio* during a worship service. He puts a description of the four movements on the screen:

Lectio (reading)
As Scripture is read, listen for one word/phrase.

Meditatio (thinking)
What is the appeal of that word/phrase?

Oratio (responding)
What do you want to say to God?

Contemplatio (resting)
Just sit with God.

George, or another worship leader, reads a passage out loud two times, and then allows five to eight minutes of silence for congregation members to engage with the four movements. Congregation members have responded very well, telling him stories about the ways God has met them through the *lectio*. Occasionally George has found it amusing that he spends so much time preparing sermons, yet sometimes God speaks to his congregation members more profoundly during a brief *lectio* before the sermon rather than in the sermon itself.

Some members of George's congregation are applying the pattern of reflection learned in *lectio divina* to other areas of Christian life. George recounted a recent conversation:

> Because *lectio divina* calls people to listen for that one word/phrase and meditate on that, I think it is becoming a way people engage with sermons. Just last Sunday after I preached, a member of the congregation came up and said, "You know how you tell us to listen for that one thing? Well, in the sermon today I did." In my sermon I had spoken about "Hollywood Theology" and how Christians can believe the silliest things about death. For instance, often people talk about the deceased still being with them and watching over them. In my sermon I said "It is God who is with you. It is God who is watching over you. Not your loved one." This congregational member, who is all of eighty years old, went on to say that he has always maintained his dead mother was watching over his shoulder and looking out for him. He said today he realized it is God, not his mother. He arrived at this by listening to the sermon, waiting for that "one word/phrase" that the Spirit can challenge him with.

Patterns of Engaging with *Lectio Divina*

The experience of George's congregation members reveals some of the significance of *lectio divina*. As an approach to Scripture, it encourages us to listen for God to speak to us. It enables us to allow Scripture and God's truth to interrogate our lives. Because we are invited to reflect on the phrase or word that shimmers for us, God's Spirit, working through the Scripture passage, can help us to see the patterns of our own lives in the light of God's truth. We might see that something we have believed simply isn't true, like the elderly man in George's congregation. We might find, as I did, that our love for jewelry—or electronics, food, entertainment media, sex, or any other aspect of modern life—needs to be viewed in a new way, as less important than God's Living Bread that comes down from heaven in Jesus.

Like so many other contemplative prayer practices, many people find it easier to wait in silence in company with others rather than alone. I enjoy *lectio* in a group setting for two main reasons. First, engaging in silence in a group enables me to sit in silence longer, so I get more out of the passage. Secondly, I love the sharing afterwards. I am usually amazed by the diversity of aspects of a passage that other people have contemplated, and the variety of ways they have heard from God. As Elizabeth and Jonathan noted, *lectio* has helped me respect the faith journey of people with whom I disagree on some particular issue.

The various examples given in this chapter illustrate the way that many leaders couple *lectio* with something else, such as another contemplative prayer practice, communion, inductive Bible study, corporate worship, or a business meeting. *Lectio divina* is one of many ways of engaging with the Bible, and any setting where a Bible passage might be read or a Bible-based devotion given can be an appropriate venue for an experience of *lectio*. Sometimes *lectio* is followed by communion, with the *lectio* standing in the place of the Scripture reading and exposition of Scripture that is typical before communion.

In any setting with a significant amount of time available for reflective activities, *lectio* can be an excellent prelude to another form of contemplative prayer, such as centering prayer, because it provides a foundation in Scripture for the time of silence. Some practitioners are adamant that Scripture, perhaps in the form of *lectio*, must precede any experience of contemplative prayer, so that God's Word is a foundation for reflection and prayer.

In contrast, other leaders like to engage in centering prayer or other forms of silent prayer *before* the *lectio divina*. This pattern works well because contemplative prayer opens participants' hearts to hear God's voice, which lays a foundation for approaching Scripture. Sometimes we have a hard time putting ourselves into a posture of listening. Spending time quieting our hearts and settling into a reflective place through breath prayer, *examen*, a guided meditation, or centering prayer can teach us to listen more closely to God's Word and the movement of God's Spirit in us when we finally do get to the *lectio*.

> Lectio divina *is not a methodical technique for reading the Bible. It is a cultivated, developed habit of* living *the text in Jesus' name.*
>
> —Eugene Peterson,
> *Eat This Book*

Like all contemplative prayer practices, *lectio* invites a particular kind of conversation afterwards. The sharing focuses on insights gained and God's word speaking into an individual's life, not on analysis, argumentation, or trying to convince someone of something. All the people who spoke with me about communal *lectio divina* affirmed the significance of this kind of conversation, saying it helps us grow in our ability to talk deeply about faith issues and in trusting that others have an authentic experience of God. My own experience echoes these comments. I have observed that this kind of conversation helps us listen to diverse experiences of God's presence with us and to discern communally what God is doing in our midst and how we might be invited to join in.

Because *lectio divina* centers on the Bible and hearing God's Word to us, it can be a significant spiritual practice for those who want to live more missionally. God's Word reveals God's priorities. The more we let God speak to us through that Word, the more we will understand, appreciate, and care about God's goals and perspectives. Because everyone engaging in the *lectio* may be able to hear from God, *lectio* is a wonderful way to increase participation in the mission of God in the world around us.

Ignatian Gospel Contemplation

When Elizabeth and Jonathan lead *lectio divina*, they sometimes ask participants to imagine themselves in the scene. Those instructions do not come from Guido, writing in the twelfth century. They come from Ignatius of Loyola in the sixteenth century.

When my sons were very small, I enjoyed reading a particular children's book to them. The book told the Christmas story from the point of view of a mouse who was there in the stable, watching Mary and Joseph, the animals, the shepherds, and, most of all, Jesus. I had no idea at that time that the book was drawing on a pattern of reflection called Ignatian Gospel Contemplation, in which we imagine ourselves as participants in a Gospel story.

Throughout Christian history, long before Ignatius in the sixteenth century, many Christians undoubtedly found great benefit from imagining themselves being present in scenes from the Bible, especially stories from the Gospel. The same is true today, whether or not we have ever heard of Ignatius or the phrase "Gospel contemplation." When we read or hear a Gospel story, we easily find ourselves wondering what we would have noticed if we had been there in the stable, or in the upper room, or at the foot of the cross. We picture ourselves as the leper receiving Jesus' touch or as the woman who touched his cloak in fear and hope. Long before I learned about Ignatian Gospel Contemplation (which I'll abbreviate as IGC in this chapter), I used to picture myself in scenes where Jesus was doing something remarkable and envision the ways I would have responded.

Unlike *lectio divina*, which was designed by Guido as a self-contained activity that could stand on its own as well as accompany other forms of prayer, IGC was originally a part of the thirty-day Spiritual Exercises. These exercises were devised by Ignatius as the initial training for members of the order he established, the Society of Jesus (the Jesuits). The Spiritual Exercises' principal focus is to meditate on the life of Jesus so that the participant may discern and respond to the call of God and live according to the law of Christ.

Imagining ourselves as a part of a Gospel story is easy to do in a variety of settings such as small groups, worship services, and retreats. Unfortunately, the pattern of IGC, the precise steps laid out by Ignatius, are rarely experienced in group settings. His instructions give richness and depth to the experience, so I will lay out and describe the steps here.[2]

Preparatory Prayer. Ignatius invites us to begin with a prayer acknowledging the love of God and consciously placing ourselves in God's presence. This prayer is significant because choosing to remember and trying to accept God's love before reading the Bible lays a foundation for free imagination tainted as little as possible by negative thoughts about ourselves.

First Prelude: Subject Matter. We choose and read a story from the Bible, usually from one of the Gospels, reading out loud if possible, and reading the passage three to five times, or as many times as it takes to absorb the content.

Second Prelude: Composition of Place. Ignatius encourages us to engage

> *Ignatius would say we draw on the five senses to be present. So that later, after prayer, we are present even to that person walking by whom we would otherwise dismiss or ignore.*
>
> —Fr. John O'Connor, quoted in Geoff New's *Back to the Future*

our senses with respect to the story. What would the scene look like up close and from a distance? What smells or sounds might be present? If someone is touching something or someone, what might it feel like? If someone is eating, what might the food taste like?

In many settings, when we are invited to imagine a scene from the Bible, we stop after this step, and certainly any passage of the Bible is more vivid to us if we can engage our senses as we imagine it. However, the genius of Ignatius's approach is that he invites us to dwell in the passage much further.

Third Prelude: Asking for the Desired Grace. Before spending more time imagining the scene, this step encourages us to identify exactly what we are hoping for as we contemplate the scene further, and to ask God for that specific grace. Geoff New writes about this prelude:

> Throughout the Exercises the desired grace asked for ranges from asking for "an intimate knowledge of our Lord" to asking for "sorrow, compassion and shame because the Lord is going to his suffering for my sins." The specific grace requested will vary from person to person, depending on the material being contemplated and the current circumstances the person is experiencing.[3]

The desired grace flows from reading the passage and engaging the senses as a participant visualizes the passage. The desired grace needs to be in keeping with the spirit of the passage. It would be inappropriate, for example, to pray for the grace of experiencing joy when contemplating a passage focused on the suffering of Jesus, or to pray for a renewed sense of sin and shame when contemplating the resurrection.

In New's research, in which he trained preachers to use both *lectio divina* and IGC in sermon preparation, this third prelude proved to be significant to many of his participants.

The Third Prelude removed some of the tensions and fixed expectations of the experience, and enabled participants to identify the grace they did receive, even if it was different than what they expected. I wonder if we miss a great deal of depth when we invite people to imagine themselves in a Gospel passage because we skip this step.

Contemplation. Only after the three preludes can the true contemplation begin. In this step, we use our imagination to identify with a particular character in the story. We can also observe the story as if we were standing to one side, engaging with the events and the other people present. We sink into the story as deeply as we can, for as long as we can. Some people find it helpful to imagine running the story through their minds like a movie. A typical tendency when pondering a Gospel story is to revert to analyzing our own situation: "I wish I had the same kind of faith as that person in the story," or "I should be able to approach Jesus like that woman did." Try releasing those analytical and self-critical thoughts by using the metaphors described in the previous chapter. Think of self-recriminations as leaves floating by on a river, boats that we need to refrain from climbing onto. Despite distractions like noises coming from outside a window, our focus is on our friend, Jesus, here in the room with us. The focus of the contemplation time is to be with Jesus, in the Gospel story, as deeply and completely as we can.

Colloquy or Conversation. After the contemplation, Ignatius encourages us to have a conversation with Jesus as a friend speaking to another friend, focused on whatever we want to say after the contemplation. The conversation should be honest and forthright. Again, we need to release our sense of what we should be or say or do. Instead, we seek an honest discussion with Jesus of what we have experienced as the priority for this time.

Most of the time, when we are invited in group settings to imagine ourselves in a biblical passage, the time involved is brief. Any engagement of the imagination can be helpful, but I believe we miss much of the potential richness of

IGC because we don't dwell in the passage long enough. I have described in detail the steps recommended by Ignatius because I would love to see groups of Christians use his steps in contemplative settings.

Cultural Shifts

Both *lectio divina* and IGC have cognitive elements to them. They have a structure. They require that we engage our minds. In the second movement of *lectio* and in all three preludes of IGC, we need to do some thinking. These are not offhand, nonchalant, or slipshod practices. They require a posture of receptivity and attentiveness, along with a willingness to persevere in waiting for God to speak. At the same time, neither of these contemplative approaches to the Bible gives priority to the mind. Equally important are imagination, emotion, sensory experience and receptivity to God's voice and presence in any form. Talking honestly to God, whether our thoughts are logical or not, plays a role in both of these practices.

These ancient forms of engagement with Scripture are appropriate and helpful in the midst of the cultural shifts we are experiencing in our time. For much of the twentieth century, the Christian churches in the West were deeply influenced by a rational approach to faith and practice. Explaining things clearly and logically was given priority in many settings, and we lost an understanding that our lives consist of much more than our brains. God works in ways far beyond intellectual comprehension. In this postmodern, post-Christendom

> *So often we come to the text and take it apart, as if meaning lay in the pieces. Instead, we ought to let the text take us apart.*
>
> —Mary Ellen Ashcroft, from an interview by Kimberlee Conway Ireton[4]

world, these two ancient prayer/Scripture practices provide a way to keep Jesus Christ at the forefront while involving our whole being in an encounter with Jesus. We love him with heart, soul, mind, and strength.

Every part of who we are, our whole being, can be brought into God's presence in *lectio divina* and Ignatian Gospel Contemplation, including the parts of us that love jewelry, TV, sports, novel reading, films, cooking, snorkeling, or sky diving. God can speak to us in fresh ways about the patterns of our lives. Meeting God through these two prayerful approaches to the Bible can help us honor and serve God with our hearts, minds, emotions, and bodies.

Questions for Reflection, Discussion, or Journaling

1. Spend some time pondering Psalm 1:1–3, printed at the beginning of the chapter. When you think of delighting in the law of the Lord and meditating on it, what comes to mind? Do you in any way already meditate on God's Word?

2. Have you experienced *lectio divina* or Ignatian Gospel Contemplation? What was the experience like for you? What aspects were enjoyable? What aspects were challenging?

3. If you have never experienced *lectio divina* or Ignatian Gospel Contemplation, what parts of this chapter seemed inviting and interesting to you? Can you imagine introducing either of these contemplative approaches to Scripture in your small group or congregation? What would be the obstacles? What might be the benefits?

4. Spend some time pondering your experience of hearing God speak through the Bible. In what ways and in what settings do you hear God speak to you through Scripture? What feelings do you associate with reading the Bible and listening for God's voice in it? Do you have guilt associated with your engagement with the

Bible? Are joy, peace, and gratitude associated in your mind with Bible reading? Spend some time praying about your patterns of engagement with the Bible.

5. Like contemplative forms of prayer, both *lectio divina* and Ignatian Gospel Contemplation involve long periods of silence. Even if, when reading the previous chapter, you engaged with the question of the role of silence in your life, do it again now. What does silence feel like for you? In what ways and in what settings is your experience of silence rich, fruitful, challenging, difficult, or impossible? In what ways would you like to grow in your ability to embrace silence? With whom might you do that?

For Further Reading

Barry, William A. *Letting God Come Close: An Approach to the Ignatian Spiritual Exercises*. Chicago: Loyola Press, 2001. Barry directed the Spiritual Exercises for over thirty years and draws on his wisdom about the Exercises. Ignatian Gospel Contemplation is a focus for a part, not all, of the book.

Brackley, Dean. *The Call to Discernment in Troubled Times: New Perspectives on the Transformative Wisdom of Ignatius of Loyola*. New York: Crossroad, 2004. This winsome book on Ignatius describes the Spiritual Exercises as a whole, which means Ignatian Gospel Contemplation is a part, not the whole, of the book.

Casey, Michael. *Sacred Reading: The Ancient Art of Lectio Divina*. Liguori, MS: Triumph, 1997. In this practical guide, Casey presents *lectio divina* as a relevant practice in an age of individualism.

Pennington, Basil M. *Lectio Divina: Renewing the Ancient Practice of Praying the Scriptures*. New York: Crossroad, 1998. Pennington calls *lectio divina* "a way of friendship" wherein we pay attention to "the love letters from the Lord" (from the cover text).

6

HOSPITALITY

Do not neglect to show hospitality to strangers, for by doing that some have entertained angels without knowing it.
—Hebrews 13:2

Be hospitable to one another without complaining.
—1 Peter 4:9

I was raised by a mother with a distinct and significant gift of hospitality. My childhood memories are full of parties and dinners that my mom hosted. She was and is an excellent cook, and her extroverted and warm relational style helps people feel welcome in her home. In my childhood, hospitality always involved a fairly structured give and take. "We owe the Smiths and the Browns a dinner," my mother would say. Soon the Smiths and the Browns would be invited over for a meal, or they would be included in the guest list for a party. My parents' pattern of keeping track of hospitality, so no debt would be incurred, is one view of hospitality that continues to shape many people's perspective today.

Another common use of the word today is the "hospitality industry," the vast network of resorts, hotels, bed and breakfast inns, cruise ships, bus tours, boat excursions, and every other possible agency that caters to tourists. This sense of the word "hospitality" involves an exchange of money accompanied by expectations—even demands—for a level of quality commensurate with the amount of money involved.

I went into adult life with those two perspectives on hospitality in the forefront of my mind. God has reshaped my understanding of hospitality as I have learned about and experienced the generosity of God shown so abundantly in Jesus. Hospitality is no longer simply a tit-for-tat exchange of meals and lodging. In addition, it has become an opportunity to meet the risen Christ in the lives of others. Hospitality as a significant component of congregational ministry is undergoing a renaissance and a reshaping in our time as congregations explore new directions for ministry in this post-Christian, postmodern world. Congregations are finding joy in eating meals with other members, neighbors, people in need, children, and seniors. They are hosting large hospitality events for the wider community. Congregational leaders are discovering that they understand God's call to their churches more clearly when they talk casually over food with people both within and outside the congregation. Eating together breaks down barriers and builds intimacy more quickly than just about anything else.

The Bible teaches us how to be hospitable, from beginning to end.

—Henry G. Brinton,
The Welcoming Congregation

Both the Old and New Testaments encourage hospitality, but one story has shaped my understanding more than any other. On the day of Jesus' resurrection, a disciple named Cleopas and another person—perhaps a friend, a sibling, or Cleopas's wife—left Jerusalem before news of the resurrection reached them. Both of them had been eager followers of Jesus, and they walked home to Emmaus disconsolate and discouraged because Jesus had died. A stranger on the road joined their discussion, asking them why they were sad. They told him about Jesus, their hopes about his kingdom, and the dashing of those hopes at his crucifixion. The stranger, extremely well-versed in Jewish history and the Hebrew Scriptures, told them his perspective about the life and work of the Messiah.

When Cleopas and his companion reached their home in Emmaus, they invited the stranger in for a meal. When the visitor broke bread at the table and blessed it, they knew instantly that this was Jesus, now resurrected and still alive. After their moment of recognition, he vanished. They thought back to the conversation on the road, and realized the thrill of hearing him explain his own mission in his own words. "Were not our hearts burning within us while he was talking to us on the road, while he was opening the scriptures to us?" (Luke 24:32).

These disciples invited a stranger into their home for a meal. They were the hosts, the ones who asked him in, but at the table this guest turned things upside down. The stranger broke the bread and blessed it, becoming the host. Like Cleopas and his companion, congregations today are increasingly exploring ways to provide hospitality to strangers. As they do, they are experiencing the presence of Jesus, who is present in friend and stranger. God invites us to extend the rich welcome that we ourselves have been offered, an invitation that shines through on page after page of the Bible. After a brief look at a small portion of the biblical material on hospitality, this chapter will relate stories of some small and large acts of hospitality in congregations.

Hospitality in the Bible

Hospitality plays a role in the Bible from beginning to end. The Jewish sacrificial system involved contributions of food that were consumed in festivals in the Temple. Some of Jesus' most memorable encounters with individuals occur in the context of hospitality in people's homes. Two examples are his discussion with Mary and Martha about the "one needful thing" while Martha was preparing a meal (Luke 10:38–42) and Jesus' extension of loving grace to an outcast woman who washed his feet with her tears in the middle of a dinner (Luke 7:36–50). Several of Jesus' parables present vivid pictures of feasts; one example is the parable of the great wedding feast in Matthew 22:1–14. Furthermore, in his last meal with his disciples, Jesus invited them to adopt a celebration of remembrance and presence that involves bread and wine.

New Testament believers viewed hospitality as an essential component of ministry. In 1 Timothy, the good works attributed to bishops and widows above reproach include hospitality (1 Tim. 3:2 and 5:10). Being hospitable also occurs throughout the Epistles in lists of recommended behavior (see Rom. 12:13 as well as the verses at the beginning of this chapter).

However, the biblical invitation to engage in hospitality goes far beyond specific verses that command it or stories that illustrate it. The deepest invitation to engage in acts of hospitality and welcome comes from the sweep of biblical history that shows the actions of a generous and hospitable God. This history began with God's invitation to Adam and Eve to dwell in the garden, and to abstain from eating one particular food. Adam and Eve violated this act of hospitality on God's part, and the rest of biblical history is the account of God's continual invitation and welcome to the people God created in love. In the incarnation we see Jesus, who came as a stranger to earth, but showed a profound welcome to the people he encountered.

It is no accident that two of the postresurrection stories involve Jesus acting as host. In the Emmaus story, Jesus begins as a stranger and guest, but then is revealed to be the host of the meal. In the incident on the beach in Galilee, Jesus helps the disciples catch fish and then cooks it for them (John 21:1–14). Both of these stories are a culmination of the generous and hospitable earthly life of the Son of God. Jesus was hospitable in spirit before his death, speaking with honor and respect to outcasts, and he demonstrated hospitality in concrete forms—involving bread and fish—after his resurrection. We are invited to go into the world with the same spirit and goals that Jesus had (John 17:18). Sometimes we are stranger and guest, and sometimes we are host. Sometimes our hospitality involves food and sometimes we act hospitably in our words or other deeds. In all roles, we are called to be open to the people we encounter in a spirit of hospitality and welcome that reflects the generosity of the God who has welcomed us.

Congregational Hospitality in Homes

Terri, the wife of a minister, is adamant about the significance of hospitality for congregations. She remembers driving across the United States when she was fifteen years old. One Sunday in Pennsylvania, she and her family attended a Mennonite church, randomly selected because of its location on their route.

After the worship service, an older couple approached Terri's family

> *Christians welcome strangers as we ourselves have been welcomed into God through the love of Jesus Christ. Through hospitality, Christians imitate God's welcome.*
>
> —Diana Butler Bass, *Christianity for the Rest of Us*

and said, "Every Sunday a family in the church is given the honor of hosting all visitors to the church for lunch. So we'd like to invite you to our home."

Terri and her family were enfolded into a clan. The home was filled with the lovely matriarch and patriarch, their adult children and spouses, and a raft of grandchildren. Terri remembers a long, leisurely afternoon on a farm, cooking, eating, sharing stories, and asking questions about what it meant to be Mennonites and how they lived.

Terri carried this spirit of hospitality with her into adulthood. In the first church where she and her husband served, they noticed a family who had a gift for hospitality. They asked this couple to host a dinner several times, inviting groups of people from the congregation to the various dinners. Terri observed that this had a bonding effect on the congregation, which she said "had never gathered much outside of worship."

Another person committed to hospitality in homes is Doug, a Presbyterian minister who recently took a new position in a large urban congregation. Soon after his arrival, a new members' class was held. Eighteen people wanted to explore membership and had signed up for a class that was held on a Friday night and all day Saturday. In the past the class had always been held at church, but Doug and his wife decided to invite the class members to their house for dinner on Friday evening. The class would then continue on Saturday in a room at the church building. This Friday night dinner was the first time ever that a new members' class had involved an invitation to come to someone's home. Doug observed that "being in a home helped to create an environment where eighteen people who did not know each other could begin to connect personally. On Saturday, everything was different from having been together that way, in a home."

Doug is a firm believer in the significance of hospitality in ministry. In one of his previous churches, in Minnesota, he observed that some people in the congregation had gone to church with each other for decades but had never been in each other's homes. Doug believes that many factors, including Scandinavian reserve, contributed to a reluctance to reach out and offer hospitality. "People hadn't had a role model for doing hospitality. If it hasn't been done before, then we need to model it and talk about it. Yes, hospitality is a gift of the Spirit, but it is also a choice of the will. People can learn to become more comfortable extending hospitality."

Hosting the Wider Community

In the mid-1990s, an urban Presbyterian congregation in a major American city built a new fellowship hall. The fellowship hall was right next door to an old house, with the neighborhood food bank hosted in the garage and basement of the house. The food bank was open on Wednesdays in the late afternoon.

Soon after the new fellowship hall was completed, several church members happened to be sitting in the fellowship hall in the late afternoon on Wednesday, watching the food bank patrons coming and going. One of the church members said, "What if we hosted a meal every Wednesday for the people who come to the food bank? And what if we encouraged people from the congregation to attend the meal as well, so it could become a place where people connect with each other, not just a place where we're giving something to people in need?"

The dinner began small but quickly grew. The homeless population of the city soon found out about a free meal being offered each week, so a good number of homeless people joined the congregation members and food bank patrons. The congregation members who attended the dinner tried hard to listen to the people they met. Their listening resulted in many specific endeavors connected to the dinners, such as collecting and distributing warm clothes in the fall and toothbrushes at other times of the year.

Church members talked with neighborhood supermarket managers, who agreed to contribute food that was beyond its sell-by date. Some of that food was used to prepare the dinners, and some simply given away at the dinners.

Most of the funds for the food came from the church budget. Volunteers signed up to cook and host the dinner once a month, becoming competent at preparing meals for a couple hundred people. Many of the volunteers were members of the church, but some came from other congregations or community groups.

Some individuals, couples, elders, and home groups within the church made a commitment to attend weekly or monthly. Jonathan and his wife were one of those couples. They had been youth group leaders, and when the time came for them to leave that responsibility, they decided to commit themselves to the dinner. "We never helped in the kitchen or with take down. We simply sat at the table and talked with whoever was there. We developed some friendships with people we never would have known otherwise. It was so good for my wife and me. We love to do ministry and lead things together. This involved no planning ahead, and for the first time in our marriage we were not in a leadership role."

Jonathan has observed that something profound happens when people eat together as equals. "It was so freeing to be with people and eat together with no agenda. It was freeing because we would come and have normal conversation. We weren't the empowered ones, deigning to spend time with disempowered people. It felt like an exchange was happening, an organic process. I learned that you can talk to people without needing to try to solve their problems."

> *Often, often, often goes the Christ in the stranger's guise.*
>
> —Celtic saying, quoted in Ronald Ferguson's *Chasing the Wild Goose*

Jonathan cited Henri Nouwen, who wrote, "Hospitality . . . means primarily the creation of a free space where the stranger can enter and become a friend instead of an enemy. Hospitality is not to change people, but to offer them space where change can take place."[1] Jonathan believes that the church members hosting the Wednesday dinner have learned that truth. He also feels that the church community learned important lessons through the relationships that were nurtured. "People had to learn the freedom to say no to requests. You have to have that freedom in order to say yes with authenticity."

Over time, some of the food bank patrons and homeless people who attended the dinner made efforts to contribute. A few played the piano or jumped in to help with clean up. And, after the dinner had been going a few years, some people from the food bank and homeless communities began to attend the worship service, changing the upper-middle-class demographic of the congregation.

After the dinner had been going for about seven years, the food bank closed its doors for numerous reasons. However, the dinner was so firmly established that it continued without missing a beat. Around the same time, church leaders decided to hire a part-time social worker to be available to the people who attended the dinner. Members and leaders who had been attending the dinner had heard many stories of struggle in finding housing and jobs, and they wanted to provide some practical help. Congregational leaders had begun to realize that housing and jobs were harder to come by for many people than food was, so they decided to put their resources into a social worker rather than into the food bank. Some of the new members of the congregation had housing and job needs as well. The congregational and dinner communities continued to spill over into each other in challenging and exciting ways with the addition of the social worker.

Doug, who served the congregation as senior pastor for eleven years (from the third to the fourteenth year of the dinner's existence), noted, "We opened ourselves up and learned that people who are having a tough time are still people. We learned that hospitality can be costly. But welcoming changes the heart of the welcomers."

Doug was very aware of a variety of safety issues at the dinner. Regarding guests' emotional safety to let down and be themselves, Doug said, "A good number of street people communicated with us that they experienced the dinner as a safe place because they had been welcomed. Maybe they could think about other risks like permanent housing. The safety and welcome of the dinner made other ministry possible."

When the dinner participants referred to the safety of the event, they weren't referring only to emotional safety. The risks of hospitality can be very real in the area of physical safety as well, particularly because of the high level of mental illness and addiction among street people. Two church members, older women with a passion for prayer, came to the church building every week at the time of the dinner and sat in a quiet room praying throughout the duration of the dinner hour. Their prayers, along with the prayers of the volunteers from the congregation who attended the dinner, contributed to the safe atmosphere. Doug noted, "The level of safety at the dinner was a miracle. In my eleven years at the church, the worst thing that ever happened was that a punch was thrown one time, and there was a vocal altercation. We had to walk a few people out the door. We were very aware of the connections between the spiritual realm and physical violence."

Other Examples of Hospitality to the Wider Community

Kent, one of the church members who was involved with the Wednesday dinner described above, eventually moved overseas to work with Habitat for Humanity. In his new city, he has tried to create a similar dinner, "born of a desire to create a setting wherein marginalized and homeless people can relax and dine together with people who are integrated into the community in order to facilitate friendships that benefit everyone." The group organizing the dinner recruited churches, businesses, civic organizations, and social groups to prepare and serve at least one community dinner. They hope that they can bring friendship, music, normalcy, and beauty into the lives of marginalized people on a regular basis.

Jonathan, mentioned above, is now the minister of a mid-sized, mostly white congregation in a multi-racial neighborhood. His congregation decided to try to get to know their neighbors by hosting an all-you-can-eat barbecue on the front lawn on a busy street for one dollar. "We wanted to tell our neighbors that we're here, we love Jesus, we're not scary, and we're interested in our neighborhood." They set the fee at a dollar in order to avoid the fear of free food. "People are sometimes wary of free food—like there will be strings attached, or we'll force them into a Bible study or something. We didn't need the one dollar, we just wanted people to have buy-in and not feel like they owed us something." To their total surprise, more than a thousand people showed up, and they had planned for only three to four hundred. They had to make four additional runs to Costco for food. Jonathan was very pleased with the conversations he was able to have that day, saying "I met more of our neighbors that day than in my previous ten months of pastoring here." Later that year the church decided to sponsor a safe trick-or-treating event in their parking lot, hosted out of car trunks, with the goal of communicating "we care about you and the safety of your kids." Again there was a good turnout from the neighborhood.

Another small congregation in a major city has taken a very different approach to offering hospitality to the wider community. They recruit chefs and people who are willing to offer their houses to host a meal. The chefs prepare meals related to their favorite food choices—a cheese meal, a chocolate-themed meal—and congregation members invite friends and others from the community. Everyone who attends pays whatever they consider to be appropriate for the meal. The minister of the church has been pleased with the variety of people who attend. "We have a mix of our people at church who come and new people," he related. "We don't seem to have many problems finding new people who want to join. Benefits have been for our people to sit down and have a meal with people who don't believe the same things they do and work out how to relate." The biggest recruitment problem has proven to be finding houses where the meals can be held. "As far as chefs go, there are people lining up wanting to have a go at their particular food choice."

The Multicultural Congregation

Many congregations rent space to other congregations who "nest" in the church building. This involves letting a congregation, often composed of immigrants, rent space for a separate worship service. The range of connection between the host congregation and the nesting congregation goes from almost no contact at all to occasional contact to various attempts to build significant relationships between the congregations. All congregational nesting arrangements—across the range of possibilities—are an opportunity to learn new patterns of hospitality.

A small congregation in California has welcomed Chinese immigrants from the neighborhood. Rather than nesting, this congregation has experimented with blended worship, trying to figure out ways each group can be authentically who they are and yet also be together.

At 9:45 on Sunday mornings, everyone arrives. The Chinese members of the congregation begin their service in Mandarin, with singing, a sermon, and prayers. The English-speaking members of the congregation gather for

Christian education for adults and children. At 10:45, the English-speaking congregation processes into the worship space to join the Chinese group, and for thirty minutes everyone remains together to enjoy prayers, songs, and an anthem performed by the choir—in a mix of English and Mandarin. They pass the peace. Then the Mandarin-speaking congregation leaves for children's and adult Christian education and the English-speaking group stays in the worship space for a sermon.

After worship and Christian education, everyone has lunch together. One of the Chinese families owns a restaurant, and they often cater lunch for the whole group. The Chinese congregation celebrates Chinese festivals, and it invites the English-speaking congregation to participate. However, the hospitality goes both ways. The English-speaking members of the congregation have extended hospitality to this immigrant group that lives in their neighborhood, and have done their best to welcome them. Both groups are sometimes hosts and sometimes guests. One participant in this congregation noted, "It's very challenging to do this. You have to believe we belong together."

With the significant population shifts occurring throughout the world, multicultural connections will increasingly be a significant component of hospitality. In addition to various church nesting arrangements, some congregations are providing hospitality for immigrant groups by offering English language lessons and help with job skills, such as writing resumes and dressing for interviews. One urban congregation provided a venue for arts and music events for a local immigrant community, and another urban congregation hosted an annual art show with exhibits from the three Abrahamic faiths: Christianity, Judaism and Islam. This art show built bridges across these communities more than anything else the congregation had attempted. Some congregations are interviewing immigrant groups to identify their needs, with the intention of reaching out in various ways to help, as well as learning from them. Whatever the specific activity, the fluid movement between guest and host that Jesus shows in the Emmaus story is a common experience when relating to people from other cultures. We learn so much even as we try to provide help and hospitality.

Sunday Morning Hospitality

Charles, a Presbyterian minister, believes that many churches fall down in the fairly simple matter of extending hospitality at worship services. "Many churches have done away with greeting at the door, introductions, and fellowship afterwards. Recently while on holiday, I was asked to move because I was 'in someone's seat'! New people are often ignored because many churchgoers feel that it is not their job or 'calling' to speak to others."

Hospitality on Sunday morning is a crucial aspect of a congregation's reflection of the welcome of Jesus Christ. Many of the hospitality issues related to worship services are revealed as a congregation begins to host people from the wider community. At a community-wide dinner, perhaps some participants can't find the bathrooms. This raises the question of whether Sunday morning visitors can find them, and new signage may need to be posted. At another community-wide event, some of the participants ask questions about the congregation that is hosting the event. "Who are you, anyway? Why are you doing this?" Questions like that reveal the need for a clear presentation of the congregation's identity and values in a brochure and on the

> *Unfortunately, we often go to church with the attitude of a guest, not a host — we are concerned more about ourselves than about those who visit with us.*
>
> —Henry G. Brinton,
> *The Welcoming Congregation*

congregation's Web site.[2] At another event, the lobby area is overly crowded as people enter and leave. Therefore, the congregation's leaders take a fresh look at ways to unclutter that space and make it more welcoming.

Charles's astonishing story of being asked to leave "someone's seat" illustrates some of the consequences of a lack of welcome during the worship service. However, being hospitable on Sunday mornings begins long before the worship service. The place of worship communicates profoundly. Are the exterior of the building and the grounds attractive and tidy enough to be welcoming? If there is an exterior sign, does it give accurate information in a welcoming way? As people enter the building, do they walk into a welcoming space, free from extraneous clutter? Is the lighting bright? If they need a bathroom, will they be able to find it easily?

I teach a course on ministry and communication, and I sometimes suggest to my students that they help their congregations engage in a "communication audit." My students are mostly older, and almost all are engaged in congregational ministry in some form. I suggest they look at everything about their church that communicates in any way—the building, paper publications, e-mails, Web site, phone answering system, signage, as well as the worship service—through the eyes of a visitor. Some of my students have reported back how helpful it was to try to look at everything through different eyes. They were amazed at the deficiencies and inconsistencies they observed.

That same exercise of pretending to be a newcomer can be instructive during a worship service. Are visitors welcomed without being put on the spot to do something uncomfortable? Are things explained in ways that would be clear to a visitor? Does the printed bulletin help worshipers know when to stand and sit? Will visitors feel uncomfortable pressure to contribute to the offering? Consider gathering together a group of people to do a thorough communication audit of your congregation. You'll be amazed at the many little things you notice that could be tweaked to communicate a warmer welcome. Perhaps you'll notice major issues as well.

As Charles noted, someone to greet people before the service is essential. What happens after the service can also go a long way to reflect a congregation's hospitable spirit. I know of two ministers who encourage the people in their congregations to spend three minutes after the worship service talking with someone they don't know. Both ministers frequently give verbal encouragement to worshipers to do this, and they urge the congregation to embrace this practice even when not reminded.

Sarah, a seminary professor, is very aware of the challenge of communicating a personal welcome in a large congregation. Yet she knows it can be done. "One time I went to a giant Anglican church. I was blown away by the people who reached out to me and talked to me. It was a church with formal architecture, a formal liturgy, and an upper-middle-class flavor. In another big church the elders and deacons are asked to commit to a service and come early or stay late to reach out to new people."

Henry G. Brinton visited several churches known for their hospitality, and he recounts what he observed in a wonderful book called *The Welcoming Congregation*. Brinton makes the point that one of the transitions many congregational members need to make is to grow in viewing themselves as hosts at the worship service, rather than participants, guests, or consumers.[3] This changes the perspective from, "What am I getting out this?" to "How can I welcome people?" This shift has far-reaching implications because it changes the tone of our participation in Sunday worship. We have come to meet Jesus Christ, and perhaps we will meet him in a conversation with someone we've never seen before.

Holding a coffee hour before or after a worship service provides perhaps the most basic opportunity for hospitality.

Recently my students engaged in a spirited online discussion about the role of coffee hour in a missional focus for a congregation. They had scathing remarks for the poor-quality coffee and cookies that are so often offered at coffee hour. Several of them said that we talk in Christian circles about Jesus' abundant welcome, and then we provide mediocre food and drink at coffee hour, a cognitive dissonance that does not exactly welcome the stranger.

Many congregations, however, do coffee hour very well. The temptation for those churches is to imagine that they have engaged in enough hospitality. Much more can be done. Meals in homes, meals in the church building, events involving food or the arts that welcome the neighborhood, sharing space and worship with ethnic congregations . . . all of these are actions that congregations are exploring. They flow from a growing awareness of the profound welcome offered to us in Jesus Christ.

> *Many early Christian texts deliberately confuse the roles of host and guest. Particularly in stories about hospitality offered, it is sometimes hard to tell who is giving and who is receiving.*
>
> —Amy G. Oden,
> *And You Welcomed Me*

A Skill or a Gift?

I mentioned earlier that my mother has a visible gift of hospitality. Some of the interviewees for this chapter mentioned that in their churches they have identified people with the gift of hospitality, and have encouraged those people to develop and use that gift for the benefit of church members as well as people beyond the congregation. Is hospitality a gift? And should those of us who don't have that gift stand back and encourage the gifted ones to use their gift while we engage in other forms of ministry?

Christine Pohl, author of a book on hospitality that has profoundly shaped my perspective on this important topic, believes that hospitality involves several components. "Hospitality is a skill and a gift, but it is also a practice which flourishes as multiple skills are developed, as particular commitments and values are nurtured, and as certain settings are cultivated."[4] My mother has a natural gift for hospitality, but I saw it develop over my lifetime as she grew in skills. She became a better cook and developed a repertoire of delicious dishes. She improved in her ability to set a lovely table. Most significantly, she grew in confidence in welcoming people into her home. In my childhood, her hospitality usually involved only friends or my father's coworkers. As she experienced an empty nest and as her hospitality skills flourished, she began to host people she didn't know and from whom she didn't expect an invitation in return. She demonstrated an ease and comfort that came from long practice.

Pohl indicates that hospitality thrives when three things are present: the growth and development of skills, the affirmation of values and commitments, and the development of settings that make hospitality possible.[5] In the stories of congregational hospitality in this chapter, all three aspects are visible. Skills develop as hospitality is practiced. Values and commitments shape the actions that congregations engage in. And settings make a difference. Without a parking lot of the right size and shape, a trunk-or-treat Halloween experience is not possible. Without a large fellowship hall, a community dinner that serves two hundred people every week can't happen.

However, simply having a spacious parking lot or fellowship hall won't make hospitality events begin or thrive. A deep commitment to building bridges with the wider community must be present. Jennifer, a Salvation Army minister, believes that church leaders can create a climate that fosters a commitment to welcome the stranger. She reflected,

I have facilitated seminars called "Building a Climate of Love" where issues of welcome and hospitality are presented. I found if I asked the participants to think personally about how they feel entering unfamiliar situations, they are able to empathize and have more of an understanding about how new people may feel when they come to join us. I had positive feedback from my attempts to encourage people to be intentional about cultivating a welcoming climate. All that was needed was awareness and teaching.

Hospitality: Simple yet Challenging

On one of the mornings when I was writing this book, I went through my interview notes and wrote up all the stories related to hospitality that you have read in this chapter. With each successive story that I recounted, I could feel my heart lifting. I felt so encouraged by the many ways congregations are showing God's love to friends and strangers. I found myself thinking, *Hospitality is not rocket science.* Hospitality is not complicated or convoluted. It simply involves offering an honest and open welcome, often accompanied by food and drink, to the people who are nearby, people who are familiar and people not yet known. Hospitality is often about simple things freely given.

After transcribing and summarizing hospitality stories from my notes that morning, I ate lunch with my husband. He asked me what I had been doing, and I told him I'd been writing up hospitality stories. He asked me to tell him a few of them, so I did. After I told three or four stories, he got a pensive look on his face and echoed the exact words I had been thinking earlier: "You know, this isn't rocket science. Hospitality flows so straightforwardly from a desire to welcome people and show that you love them."

And yet hospitality to friend and stranger, with the expectation that Jesus will be the host of the meal, requires a shift in perspective for most people. It may not be rocket science, but it requires learning to see biblical stories in a new light. It requires that we use our imagination to become aware of what it feels like to be a stranger or an outcast. It involves growing in awareness of Jesus' presence as guest and host at our tables. It requires a shift in thinking that affirms the significance of trading hospitality back and forth the way my parents did so well and so generously, while also affirming the joys of engaging with strangers, the marginalized, and unexpected guests.

The stranger at our door can be both gift and challenge, human and divine.

—Ana María Pineda, "Hospitality"

Biblical hospitality demands a commitment to develop the settings where hospitality can flourish, the values that undergird it, and the skills that make it flow smoothly. Hospitality, as modeled by Jesus, trains us to welcome people who will challenge us and enrich us because they bring his presence into our lives in unexpected and vibrant ways.

Questions for Reflection, Discussion, or Journaling

1. When you think of the word "hospitality," what comes to mind? What patterns of hospitality did you observe in your family of origin? What were the healthy and not-so-healthy aspects of what you observed? In what ways has your understanding of hospitality shifted in your adult life? What has contributed to those shifts?

2. What have been your experiences of offering and receiving hospitality in your small group, congregation, or other Christian community? In what ways have

you experienced hospitality in a community to be life-giving? Fun? Draining?
3. How do you feel about having people in your home? What do you enjoy about it and what do you find frustrating? What are your biggest fears? What helps you overcome those fears?
4. When you think of offering hospitality to someone you don't know, how do you feel? What fears arise? What opportunities do you see? In what ways can you imagine experiencing the presence of Jesus when offering hospitality to people you don't know?
5. How can hospitality be a way to understand all Christian ministry?

For Further Reading

Brinton, Henry G. *The Welcoming Congregation: Roots and Fruits of Christian Hospitality.* Louisville, KY: Westminster John Knox Press, 2012. Brinton visited several churches that are known for their hospitality in different areas, and the vivid descriptions of his visits are among the highlights of this practical and insightful book.

Newman, Elizabeth. *Untamed Hospitality: Welcoming God and Other Strangers.* Grand Rapids: Brazos Press, 2007. Newman offers good theology and practical examples here. She argues that true hospitality is learned in worship as we become more willing to receive from God.

Nouwen, Henri J. M. *Reaching Out: The Three Movements of the Spiritual Life.* Glasgow: William Collins Sons & Co, 1976. In this eloquent classic, Nouwen describes moving from loneliness to solitude, hostility to hospitality, and illusion to prayer.

Pohl, Christine D. *Making Room: Recovering Hospitality as a Christian Tradition.* Grand Rapids: Eerdmans, 1999. This wonderful book changed my understanding of hospitality and helped me see its significance in Christian history and its value in our time.

7

SABBATH

You shall keep my Sabbaths, for this is a sign between me
and you throughout your generations, given in order that you
may know that I, the LORD, sanctify you.
— Exodus 31:13

A group of young adults in their mid-to-late-twenties gathers after church almost every Sunday. They eat lunch together, usually in a home, but sometimes in a restaurant. Then they spend the afternoon together. In dismal weather, they play board games or cards, chat and munch on popcorn. On sunny Sundays they often take a long walk at the park a couple of miles from the church. Sometimes they plan a special outing to the mountains or to a baseball game. Whatever they do, the day is relaxed and easy, focused on enjoying each other and celebrating God's gift of a restful day.

The group is conscious about calling this day, and this practice, their Sabbath. Some are married and some are single. The married couples find that these Sabbath days nurture their marriages because relaxed time together is so precious and rare. Some of them turn their cell phones off, and seldom is the TV playing. They have discovered that a break from technology helps them relax and receive the day as a gift from God.

In the years to come, more of them will marry, and some of the new spouses will take members away from the group. Some of the couples will begin to have children. At first, bringing a baby to the Sunday afternoon Sabbath gatherings is easy, but later, nap schedules and children's needs draw those parents away. After a few years, the group will morph significantly, with fewer gatherings and more Sabbaths in people's own homes with their new families. But none of them will forget those years of observing the Sabbath with a group of friends. All of them will be shaped by their memories of those relaxed Sabbaths, and they will continue to try to recapture some of the joy and peace they experienced on those restful, comfortable Sunday afternoons.

> *Rest on the Sabbath as if all your work were done. . . . Rest even from the thought of labor.*
>
> —Abraham Heschel,
> *The Sabbath*

In their early years of parenting, they will support each other as they strive to figure out Sabbath patterns that work for them in a culture permeated with an emphasis on busyness, productivity, and ceaseless activity. Over picnics with their families and in small-group Bible studies, they will discuss their Sabbath patterns, asking for advice, guidance, and prayer support as they strive to obey the fourth commandment.

The minister at their church watches them as the years pass and as they seek to obey God and keep a Sabbath. He believes the Sabbath is one of the hardest spiritual practices in our time, requiring the most creativity and diligence to make it work. He recognizes that the support these young adults give to each other has been a key factor in their ability to grow into new patterns of Sabbath keeping as their family situations change with the years.

The Sabbath at Home

In the 24/7 culture so pervasive in the Western world today, and in many other places as well, keeping a Sabbath is radical and counter-cultural. In recent years the Sabbath has come into focus for many Christians, perhaps because the increasing pace has become unsustainable. We simply don't thrive when we are scurrying around day and night.

My husband I were exposed to the Sabbath when we lived in Israel as young adults more than thirty years ago. We lived in Tel Aviv, the most Jewish of the major cities in Israel. In our neighborhood, the time between sunset on Friday and sunset on Saturday was radically different from the other days of the week. Everything was closed. And I do mean everything, including minimarts, gas stations, supermarkets, restaurants, and movie theatres. We didn't have a car, and the busses didn't run on the Sabbath. Our options were incredibly limited.

At first, the limitations of the Sabbath day felt constricting. But after a few months, a day of quiet and reduced options began to feel like a gift. Our noisy street became so quiet we could hear the voices of children playing outside. The lack of options for entertainment motivated my husband to bird watch in the vacant lot across the street, which introduced him to new and unusual birds. I wrote letters while he was gone, enjoying the gift of abundant time to get my thoughts on paper. Together we had long conversations over leisurely meals, and sometimes we prayed together without any rush. We sometimes took long walks that ended up at the home of friends. The lack of structure and the inability to go to shopping or to a movie was freeing, soothing, and life-giving.

When we returned to the United States after eighteen months in Israel, we decided to keep a Sabbath on Sundays. We wanted to keep something of the joy of a day filled with abundance, a day with reduced options for stressful activities.

Thirty years ago no other Christians we knew were keeping a Sabbath. No one was writing books or articles about the benefits of the Sabbath for Christians. We went ahead and kept our Sabbath day year after year, watching it shift and change as our children got older. We kept the basic structure of the day as the years passed: no paid work, no housework, no house repairs, and no shopping. Sunday was a day to enjoy being together as a family doing fun things, a relaxed day with no responsibilities after going to church.

In the second decade of our Sabbath observance, we began to see books and articles describing and recommending the Sabbath for Christians. Marva Dawn published the influential book *Keeping the Sabbath Wholly*, and Eugene Peterson began writing about Sabbath keeping in various places. We began to reflect on this practice that had been so important to us for so many years. We started to see the theological significance of this day that helps us remember that God runs the universe and we don't, this day in which we experience that we are beloved children of the God who created and sustains the world.

Later, more books and articles appeared, and some of them puzzled us. Some seemed to emphasize spiritual activities for the Sabbath day. It seemed that for some writers, a day of rest wasn't enough. The day needed to have a conscious spiritual focus as well. Some of those opinions came from the observation that if people don't work for a day, instead they might play video games or watch TV, and surely recreation with a compulsive component to it isn't the main point of the Sabbath.

We didn't watch TV on our Sabbath day and didn't allow our kids to watch it, and we didn't turn on our computer, so we agreed with those basic concerns about technology on the Sabbath. But we had experienced these wonderful days, full of God's grace and love, without doing very much that could be classified as "spiritual" besides going to church in the morning. We occasionally read a Bible story to our children on Sundays and we occasionally prayed together, but the day basically centered on stopping work, enjoying ourselves as a family, and engaging in hospitality from time to time. These actions, repeated week after week and year after year, had impressed on our hearts the wonderful reality that God loves us quite apart from what we do. We had learned in a nonverbal, noncognitive way the heartbeat of God's grace, and we knew more profoundly that we were beloved children of an abundantly loving Creator and Redeemer.

> *Sabbath is a time to stop, to refrain from being seduced by our desires. To stop working, stop making money, stop spending money. See what you have. Look around. Listen to your life.*
>
> —Wayne Muller, *Sabbath*

The Sabbath in the Bible

The emphasis of our Sabbath observance was (and is) stopping work, shopping, and technology. Our priorities came from the Old Testament, where stopping work is the key concept for the Sabbath. The first description of the Sabbath comes from the seventh day of creation, when God stopped working and rested (Genesis 2:2–3). The word translated "rested" comes from the same Hebrew root as the word "Sabbath," and that root means stop, cease, rest, pause, or desist.

The emphasis on ceasing work on the Sabbath day is clear in the fourth commandment. The Hebrew Scriptures contain two versions of the Ten Commandments, which were given to Moses at two different times. Most of the commandments are virtually identical between the two versions, but the one about the Sabbath varies slightly. Two different motivations are given. In the first version, the people of Israel are commanded to keep the Sabbath because God rested at creation:

> Remember the Sabbath day, and keep it holy. Six days you shall labor and do all your work. But the seventh day is a sabbath to the LORD your God; you shall not do any work—you, your son or your daughter, your male or female slave, your livestock, or the alien resident in your towns. For in six days the LORD made heaven and earth, the sea, and all that is in them, but rested the seventh day; therefore the LORD blessed the Sabbath day and consecrated it.
>
> Exodus 20:8–11

The second version of the Sabbath commandment has similar parameters. Men, women, sons, daughters, slaves, animals, and resident aliens are included in the invitation to rest. Because everyone is included, the Sabbath day is a sign of justice and mercy. In the second version of the commandment, the reason given for this invitation to rest is to celebrate freedom from slavery: "Remember that you were a slave in the land of Egypt, and the LORD your God brought you out from there with a mighty hand and an out-stretched arm; therefore the LORD your God commanded you to keep the sabbath day" (Deut. 5:15).

The two reasons given for Sabbath observance—that God rested at creation and that God freed the people of Israel from slavery—reflect two of the major roles and acts of God, our Creator and Redeemer. These two aspects of God's character can be helpful to consider when planning a Sabbath observance.

When I did interviews for my book on the Sabbath, people spoke frequently and enthusiastically about getting out in nature on the Sabbath: walking, hiking, biking, skiing, throwing a Frisbee for the dog at the beach, playing with kids at a park, or just sitting on a bench enjoying a view of the beautiful world that God created. A good number of people mentioned gardening as an enjoyable Sabbath activity. For me, gardening is work that I don't enjoy, so I would never want to garden on the Sabbath day, but I could hear real joy in the voices of some of the people I interviewed. One man mentioned going to the gym on the Sabbath because using his body in a strenuous way reminds him that God made him, body and soul.

This engagement with the physical creation fits with the first Sabbath commandment. God made the world and filled it with extravagant beauty, and God was able to rest on the seventh day because the world was amply provisioned and carefully regulated. When we enjoy the creation, we are engaging with our Creator and experiencing God's own deep joy at the wonder of this beautiful creation.

> *To act as if the world cannot get along without our work for one day in seven is a startling display of pride that denies the sufficiency of our generous Maker.*
>
> —Dorothy C. Bass,
> *Practicing Our Faith*

The second version of the Sabbath commandment addresses freedom from slavery. This idea provides another way to think about Sabbath activities. Perhaps the real downside to watching TV all day on the Sabbath is that it is addictive, so if we succumb to any addictive behavior on the Sabbath we are exchanging one form of slavery—work—for another form of slavery—addiction. Stepping outside the things that enslave us for a day will undoubtedly vary from one person to another, because we are enslaved to different things. Some people choose not to engage in multitasking on the Sabbath, because juggling two or three things simultaneously feels so tiring, and is also a form of slavery.

In the past few years, more people are talking and writing about turning off computers, cell phones, and other electronic devices on the Sabbath day. The desire to be connected electronically at all times has addictive aspects, and turning off the devices that make constant connection possible can be a step toward freedom.

Many people observe a Sabbath alone or with their family. In the opening story of this chapter, I described a group of people who have enjoyed having a Sabbath with a group of people larger than a family. Now I'll describe other models for a communal Sabbath that I have heard about. I'll begin with an individual whose Sabbath practice has influenced his congregation.

The Sabbath in Congregations

Ben, the pastor of a small congregation, is quite intentional about his Sabbath practice. He views Sundays as his Sabbath, even though he preaches and leads worship almost every Sunday. Because his church is small, he is alone quite a bit during the week, so he enjoys the contact with people on Sundays, and all the conversations on Sunday morning provide a contrast to his weekdays. Ben views contrast as a component of a Sabbath practice. The Sabbath day should be different in significant ways from the other days of the week.

Ben has several intentional practices that make his contact with parishioners different on Sundays. He tries to do everything with a spirit of appreciation. He tries to walk more slowly around the church building, observing and enjoying the building itself and all the people in it. He tries to give compliments and express his appreciation as much as he can.

"Walking slowly around the building contributes pretty consistently to an awareness of God," Ben said. "This awareness relates to God's presence in the moment, but it also relates to the enterprise of what I'm doing in my ministry and who this building really belongs to. Hustling implies that *I've* got to get things done. But I could hustle all day and work eighty hours a week, and in God's eyes that might be a failure. Walking slowly around the church building on Sundays helps me keep the big picture in mind."

Ben also tries not to conduct church business on Sunday mornings. His conversations at coffee hour focus on people: who they are, what they're thinking about, and what he can appreciate about them. He keeps church business for weekdays, including committee meetings. And if someone raises a committee issue in a conversation at coffee hour, he sets a time to talk with them about it during the week.

Congregational leaders who desire to foster a Sabbath spirit on Sundays face some serious challenges. Ben's practice of not discussing church business on Sundays illuminates one of the challenges. Talking at coffee hour about the latest development with the church budget or the permit process for the building remodel is all too easy. Scheduling a quick (or not so quick) meeting before or after church to get some business done is convenient because it removes the necessity for a meeting on another day when congregants might be busy with their regular work. But does it make the Sabbath day one more work day?

Ben has been serving the same church for more than a decade, and he has engaged in intentional Sabbath practices for about half that time. He has described those Sabbath practices to his congregation from time to time. He has noticed some changes in his flock, including a shift in the coffee-hour pattern in the years since he has been observing a Sabbath. In Ben's first years as a minister in that congregation, less than half of the people attending worship stayed for coffee hour, which was usually fairly brief. Now almost everyone who attends worship stays for coffee hour, and the time stretches on for quite a while, filled with light chat as well as deep conversations. "It's now a really sweet time of checking in with each other," Ben has noticed. "It wasn't anything we strategized about. It just shifted." Coffee hour has become a slice of Sabbath for congregation members, a relaxed time of enjoying being together, without pressure to accomplish anything, a time of laughter and rich fellowship.

> *Good sabbath-keeping includes both praying and playing. Prayerful sabbaths without play or playful sabbaths without prayer are only half-sabbaths.*
>
> — Don Postema,
> *Catch Your Breath*

For Ben, the biggest challenge in Sabbath observance for him and for several of the families in his church is Sunday sports. Ben's eleven-year-old son plays sports all year round, as do many of the other preteens and teenagers in the congregation. Many of the games are on Sundays. These families have had frequent informal conversations about the best ways to respond to the pressure that sports can put on Sundays, but they haven't come to any conclusions yet.

Many ministers choose to take a Sabbath on a weekday, which has many advantages. Ministers who find Sunday mornings exhausting can have a day of rest completely separate from the demands of leading worship and preaching. Because children are in school on weekdays, ministers with children in the home often find that weekday Sabbaths involve fewer family demands than Sundays. By comparison, Ben's choice to view Sunday as his Sabbath puts him squarely in the middle of the same issues faced by the members of his congregation. Ben needs to find a way to engage in the worship of God on Sunday, even as he leads the service and delivers a sermon. His challenge is no different than the obstacles faced by church musicians, Sunday school teachers, and a wealth of other volunteers who serve at church, who need to find a way to worship God and experience rest, even as they engage in significant service. Ben has to deal with the multiple pressures on families on Sundays, just as his parishioners do. Because he faces the same pressures, he is able to engage in creative problem-solving with the people in his congregation.

Sunday Volunteering

Anna, a church musician, gives further insight into the challenges faced by congregational volunteers. For two decades, Anna has played the guitar at church. She often leads Sunday praise music groups, and also regularly leads the singing at retreats and other church events. Music is a central way that Anna experiences God's presence, so she is grateful for her many opportunities to lead music, but she also acknowledges that most music leading involves a component of work. It requires concentration, focus, and dedication.

For many years, Anna's church had two music groups that alternated Sundays. Her church had two Sunday morning services, so on those Sundays when her group was leading, she would arrive at church at 7:30 a.m. for rehearsal, then play during the two services. She was at church for more than five hours on those Sundays.

"If I wanted to be out of town for a weekend, I could do a trade with another musician, but that filled up almost all the Sundays of a month," Anna noted. "It was particularly difficult when I went on vacation because I had to work hard before and after the vacation to free up those Sundays. It was such a relief when we changed to three music groups, so we only had to lead every third Sunday. It created more of a break for the musicians. We got so much positive feedback from the musicians. They liked being able to sit with their families more often, and they especially liked not having to arrive at 7:30 every second Sunday."

Anna believes that congregations need to do a better job thinking about the volunteers who make Sunday mornings possible, so that volunteers can have a restful Sabbath morning at least part of the time. After pondering this question, she changed the way she approached being out of town for a weekend when she was scheduled to play. Instead of trying to find someone in another music group who wanted to trade with her, she tried to find musicians who didn't play regularly but who enjoyed playing occasionally. This had two advantages. These musicians got a chance to participate, and she didn't have to "pay" for her absence by playing on another week.

Anna would like to see teams rather than individuals doing all sorts of ministry at church, such as children's and youth ministries, coffee hour, and ushering. Her own experience of two decades of music leading has given her an awareness of the privilege of any sort of church ministry, a place where she meets God and grows in relationships with other Christians. Yet that privilege is coupled with the component of work that is always present. If we believe that the Sabbath is to be a day when work stops, then we need to share the work associated with Sunday worship so everyone has some Sundays when they don't have to engage in the work of ministry.

A Weekend Sabbath

A congregation in the Midwest of the United States and a congregation in Sydney, Australia have in common that they sponsor a weekend away every year, and they call it a congregational Sabbath.

For the American congregation, the weekend is held in mid- to late-August, and the weekend is mostly unscheduled time for people to enjoy catching up on sleep and connecting with family and friends. The minister of that congregation noted that they are very conscious not to call the weekend a "retreat," which implies getting away or pulling back. They wanted the weekend to be viewed as a part of their journey to see where God is at work in a new place, a communal pilgrimage. They also wanted to use the language of "Sabbath" to capture the notion of play, rest, and worship.

> *Sabbath . . . is a time for "useless" poetry and other arts; a time to appreciate a tree, your neighbor, and yourself without doing something to them; a time to praise God as an end in itself.*
>
> —Tilden Edwards,
> *Sabbath Time*

The congregation's baptisms are held at the yearly congregational Sabbath, and the Sunday morning worship service allows people the opportunity to talk about what they have experienced. One year a man spoke during the Sunday worship and said, "I've never spent this much time playing with my children, ever."

The Australian congregation's weekend Sabbath is very similar—a weekend away at a place where they can reserve a group of cabins, with not very much activity scheduled. The minister of that church said, "What do we do? Not much. My fear was that everyone would be bored, but we found the opposite. We make sure we invite non-Christians along to see what Christians do when they are not 'doing' church, and they both love it and are intrigued by it."

He went on to say, "We see Sabbath as a time to enjoy God's order, as opposed to working to bring about God's order." The benefit of these weekend Sabbaths is to give a long block of time where people are encouraged to stop working and enjoy life in the company of others.

In our frantic 24/7 culture, many people have never slowed down long enough to unwind in the presence of God. They may have experienced leisure that involves more activities or entertainment, a form of stopping work that has refreshing aspects but is not the same as a Sabbath. For them, the weekend Sabbaths introduce something new, a time free of compulsive activity, a joyful experience of the abundance of God's provision. The Sabbath grants permission to relax and let God run the universe without our help.

In many parts of the world today, Christians generally seek to obey eight of the Ten Commandments, but two of them are routinely ignored: the Sabbath command and the command not to covet. Our neglect of these two commandments is connected. The advertising culture is grounded in the presupposition that we should covet whatever we don't have. We should want things so we will purchase them. This wanting and purchasing requires a constant state of activity, a heightened level of emotional intensity. We have to work hard to earn the money to purchase what we want, and when we stop working, we tend to feel guilty for stopping. Therefore we remain vigilant to some degree, continuing to focus on what we don't have.

This vigilance when we aren't working can take the form of shopping, which requires a continuing focus on what we don't have. Sometimes when we're not working, we engage in compulsive activities, anything from an excessive focus on entertainment to excessive amounts of food and drink. Compulsive engagement with entertainment when we're not working can at least temporarily cover up our fear that being quiet will reveal something painful, perhaps something else that we lack. By contrast, the Sabbath is a day to relax into the reality that God created an abundant universe, richly provisioned and beautifully intricate, full of people that we care about and good gifts to enjoy. Keeping a Sabbath, week after week and year after year, helps us learn to rest in God's goodness rather than think about what we imagine we are lacking.

A weekend Sabbath can introduce us to an experience of resting in the abundance of God's gifts. A weekend Sabbath should be viewed as an introduction to a pattern that can continue in a weekly form. Repetition of the Sabbath discipline of not working and not striving shapes us profoundly, and enables us to experience deep in our hearts that God loves us apart from our productivity or accomplishments.

Obstacles and Challenges

Congregational leaders will have to address numerous obstacles in order to encourage members to engage in a Sabbath practice. Some of the biggest obstacles to Sabbath keeping, as described above, are the busyness of daily life that spills over to seven days a week, and the advertisements that keep us looking for perceived holes in our collection of possessions. Those two aspects of modern life are like weeds growing with their roots entangled together. We need to engage in a lot of discussion, prayer, and study to dig up those weeds.

Other obstacles come from family of origin and theological beliefs about the Sabbath. My grandfather is an excellent example of the impact of childhood patterns on adult behavior. He was raised in a home that observed a rigid and legalistic Sabbath. My grandfather was the youngest of eight children and the only boy. By the time he came along, his older sisters had learned their father's Sabbath priority: sit still, and if you have to do something, read the Bible. Sundays were torture for my grandfather, and when he left home, he never again set foot in a church unless he had to, and he never forced his own children to sit still on Sundays. The rigidity of the Sunday Sabbaths of his childhood turned him away from anything related to God.

Congregations often have members who suffered something similar to my grandfather's experience. The word "Sabbath" conjures up memories of unpleasant days, being forced to stay indoors when other children were playing outside. In your congregation, be creative in providing opportunities for people to discuss their childhood memories of the Sabbath. Consider soliciting testimonies from people who keep the Sabbath freely and with joy.

> *When we keep the Sabbath holy, we are practicing, for a day, the freedom that God intends for all people.*
>
> — Dorothy C. Bass,
> *Receiving the Day*

Another related obstacle comes from people who believe that Jesus abolished the Sabbath and that our Sabbath rest is fulfilled in Christ. Hebrews 4 is often cited as a passage that indicates that in Christ we find our rest, not in a Sabbath observance. Congregational leaders who want to encourage Sabbath observance need to provide teaching about Jesus' miracles on the Sabbath, which reframed the purpose of Sabbath but did not abolish it. Jesus' healings on the Sabbath indicate that the day is to focus on life and health and healing, not rules. Sermons, classes, and articles for the church newsletter or Web site can explore the Old and New Testament material on the Sabbath, while emphasizing Jesus' Sabbath miracles as manifestations of God's invitation into a day that focuses on abundance, healing, and freedom.

Another challenge to Sabbath observance comes from the unfortunate reality that often we don't know how to play in a way that doesn't involve mindless entertainment. A focus on the two Sabbath commands can help congregations discuss Sabbath options that involve enjoying God's creation and experiencing freedom from the things that normally preoccupy us. An appropriate Sabbath emphasis involves resting in God as creator and enjoying the freedom from slavery given through Jesus Christ; so every Sabbath should begin with the foundation of being aware of God's goodness. A Sabbath challenge is to figure out what that looks like. In the early years of Sabbath observance for my husband, my children, and me, we attended church in the morning, which laid the groundwork for a restful day received as a gift from God.

For people who are used to being busy all the time, it can be tempting to fill up a Sabbath day with "spiritual" activities like Bible study and prayer. Discernment is necessary regarding these activities. Are they truly a gift from God and a way to draw near to God? Or, as Sabbath practices, are they part of the ceaseless activity that characterizes so much of modern life? Are they an attempt to justify ourselves in God's eyes, to prove that we deserve to be loved? Perhaps reading the Bible is exactly the right thing to do on the Sabbath, but if a person enjoys being busy, perhaps taking a hike or a long walk in a park, enjoying the beauty of the world God made, would give just as much spiritual benefit. Maybe taking a nap, as an act of acknowledgement that everything we have comes from God as a gift, might reflect our dependence on God even more.

Small groups, Bible studies, adult classes, men's and women's groups, retreats, and discussions after sermons are great places to brainstorm about what to do on the Sabbath day, and what to cease from doing. In the Jewish tradition, money should not be handled (or thought about) on the Sabbath. An interesting discussion might center on the ways life would be different without money for one day each week. Another fruitful discussion might focus on slowing down on the Sabbath. Could attendance at children's sporting events have a different flavor on the Sabbath day if everyone in the family slowed down on that day, left the house early, and didn't rush around to get to the game? How might that one day each week—even if it involved children's sports—look different if no multitasking was happening?

Another challenge for congregations is how to provide options for people to gather for Sabbath observance, while also affirming that some people may need to be alone on the Sabbath day or simply rest at home with their families. In contrast, some people are alone at work all week, and need time with other people on the Sabbath. Communal Sabbath observance usually wouldn't mean that everyone in the congregation is together all day long. The long leisurely coffee hour, where people can talk for a long time if they like, illustrates one option.

Is the Sabbath one of the hardest spiritual practices in our time? Do congregation members need support for Sabbath keeping as much or more than they need support for other ways of living out the Christian faith? If so, then the communal issues related to the Sabbath will involve much creative thinking, discussion, and prayer.

Perhaps the most important thing congregational leaders can do to encourage Sabbath observance is to talk about it and make spaces for people to brainstorm together and pray for each other. Consider encouraging all the congregation's home groups to focus on the Sabbath during Lent by reading a book or working through a Bible study guide. Consider devoting an all-church retreat to the topic of the Sabbath, or having a sermon series on the Sabbath with discussions afterward. Consider using a church newsletter or Web site to present Sabbath options or to allow Sabbath keepers within the congregation to write about their experience.

The kind of Sabbath my grandfather was subjected to, where everyone sat still all afternoon on Sunday, is only one of hundreds of options for what a Sabbath might look like. The Sabbath is a day to lay down the tools of our daily work, paid or unpaid, and to rejoice in the way God has ordered the universe, enjoy the good gifts God has given us, and receive God's love. What might that look like for members of your congregation?

Questions for Reflection, Discussion, or Journaling

1. In your family of origin or in the church of your childhood, what did you learn about Sabbath observance? What positive and negative associations do you have with the idea of Sabbath keeping?
2. What emotions do you associate with the notion of rest? Do you ever let yourself rest without feeling guilty? When you think about stopping productivity, how do you feel?
3. Have you seen any patterns of communal Sabbath observance that seem life-giving to you? Can you imagine a pattern of Sabbath observance that might be fruitful? If you currently engage in a Sabbath, what aspects of it are most life-giving for you? What are the biggest challenges?
4. What are the places and times in your life that you experience moments of communal rest from work? Perhaps these are moments when you feel joy in the abundance of the world God made, or that help you know you are not a slave to anything or anyone. In what ways is it different experiencing these moments in the presence of others rather than alone?
5. If you want to begin or continue a practice of Sabbath keeping, what sort of support do you need or would you find helpful? Can you imagine asking for that support in any of the groups of people with whom you regularly engage?

For Further Reading

Baab, Lynne M. *Sabbath Keeping: Finding Freedom in the Rhythms of Rest*. Downers Grove, IL: InterVarsity Press, 2005. My own book on the Sabbath draws on my experience and the stories of many interviewees.

Edwards, Tilden. *Sabbath Time*. Rev. ed. Nashville: Upper Room Books, 2003. This gentle and encouraging book emphasizes the Christian contemplative tradition.

Heschel, Abraham Joshua. *The Sabbath*. New York: Farrar, Straus and Giroux, 1951. An eloquent classic written by a Jewish scholar.

Muller, Wayne. *Sabbath*. New York: Bantam Books, 1999. This beautifully written book draws on traditions of rest in world religions and shows how Sabbath keeping addresses many issues of our time.

Postema, Don. *Catch Your Breath: God's Invitation to Sabbath Rest*. Grand Rapids: CRC Publications, 1997. Seven helpful meditations on aspects of Sabbath keeping for Christians, designed to be discussed in groups.

8

⬭⬭

SPIRITUAL PRACTICES
AND CONGREGATIONAL
DISCERNMENT

If we live by the Spirit, let us also be guided by the Spirit.
—Galatians 5:25

Theo is the minister of a mid-sized congregation in a multi-racial neighborhood. The congregation is at a crossroads in several ways. As this largely white congregation has watched the ethnic shifts in the community around the church, the leaders and members have found themselves wishing they could do a better job connecting with and serving the people in the neighborhood. In addition, for the past few years, attendance has been dwindling at many of the adult education opportunities offered by the church. The group life team, charged with the oversight of the adult education program, decided to suspend all new programs for a few months in order to engage in a process of discernment about the future.

In consultation with Theo, the team realized that the process of discernment needed to have a wider focus than just the adult education program. They decided to put three questions to the congregation:

— Where do you think God's heart is for our congregation?
— Where do you think God is leading our congregation?
— What would it take for you to join in?

Congregation members were invited to reflect on and pray about the questions, and then attend two discussion times where they could report on their reflections and engage in a discernment process about where God might be leading the congregation. The first congregational discussion was held on a weekday evening. The second was scheduled after the Sunday morning worship service, and congregation members were invited to fast from lunch, if they were able, in order to engage in discussion and prayer together.

Theo observed the two discussions closely and remarked, "There was a huge difference in depth between the two times. The first felt a bit perfunctory and the second felt rich, like the Spirit was moving. There was a sense of direction. We engaged in honest corporate confession of some of the pride in our past." He believes fasting made the difference. An outside observer could argue that the second discussion would most likely have been deeper than the first simply because some foundation had been laid during that first session. However, the difference was great enough that Theo is convinced that fasting during the second meeting was the key.

Consensus and Discernment

Each of the six spiritual practices described in this book can play a significant role in congregational discernment. In a time when congregations are dealing with unprecedented challenges—ethnic shifts in neighborhoods, dwindling financial resources, changes in family patterns, less time available for volunteering, and an increasingly secular society—discernment has become a central issue. What is God calling us to do? What unique contribution can we, in this specific congregation, make in our community? In the wider world?

If we want to be missional congregations, engaging with God's mission in the world, modeling ourselves after the incarnational ministry of Jesus, these questions are vital. We need to hear the Holy Spirit's guidance about exactly what we are called to do in our community and in the wider world. We need to grow in our ability to discern the difference between a good idea and the right idea, the direction where God is calling us to walk.

> *Spiritual discernment is, at its heart, the art of distinguishing what leads to God from what does not.*
>
> —Helen H. Cepero, "Models of Spiritual Discernment"

The question of discernment has come into view because of another issue as well. Many congregational leaders are tired of church organization being conducted by Robert's Rules of Order. They quite rightly rebel against a kind of dualism that views worship and small groups as spiritual, while leadership of the church is treated like business. Either God is present in everything we do, and we expect God's guidance in all our activities, or we are engaging in hypocrisy.

Some leadership boards in congregations have moved beyond Robert's Rules of Order to embrace a process of consensus building, and consensus has many advantages over voting. Consensus involves discussion, leading to general agreement about a conclusion or decision. This process is often slower than voting on a decision after only brief discussion, but it usually results in a greater degree of ownership by participants, and it provides the opportunity to deal with resistance earlier than when decisions are made by voting.

Often consensus building among congregational leaders centers on meeting the greatest number of needs or desires. The focus is on what we need and want. In contrast, discernment is radically different because it focuses on listening for God's voice and guidance through the Holy Spirit. Discernment is grounded in the presupposition that our lives and our ministry belong to God, and that God's Spirit will guide us into decisions that reflect God's will and values. Our needs and desires need to be considered, but they are neither the starting point nor the primary motivator.

Both consensus and discernment require carefully listening to everyone involved, so the process is similar. In fact, consensus plays a role in the discernment process, as a group tries to come to a conclusion about what they are together hearing from God. The kind of consensus that plays a role in discernment involves the following:

— Being willing to speak what we think we might be hearing from God
— Listening carefully to others
— Paraphrasing or summarizing what we think we hear others saying
— Making sure quiet people have the opportunity to speak
— Pausing from time to time to pray or reflect

How do we arrive at consensus through discernment? Spiritual practices help us remember who God is and who we are, an essential first step. They give a foundation for peace and resting in God. They help us keep our roots in Christ. Engaging in centering prayer or the prayer of *examen* together, practicing *lectio divina* as a leadership group, or spending a long time in thankfulness prayers can get a process of discernment off to a good start because they remind us who we are and whose we are. They remove the dualism of viewing worship as spiritual while dismissing planning as business as usual. They set the stage for a listening process.

In addition, the spiritual practices described in this book can play a role in the middle or later stages of a process of discernment. In different ways, each of these disciplines helps groups of Christians discern what God is up to, the key component of all stages of discernment. These are not the only practices that can help with discernment, but revisiting each of the six practices in turn will help illuminate the role of Christian spiritual disciplines in the practice of discernment. One church member remarked that spiritual practices are "like cleaning my glasses," restoring fresh and clear vision. Having clean glasses makes a valuable contribution to discernment at any stage.

> *Discernment has to do with identifying communications that come from God.*
>
> — Douglas McBain,
> *Eyes That See*

Thankfulness

When we spend time thanking God, we are forced to look at our lives. When we spend time thanking God as a group, we are forced to look at our communal life. We notice things that we simply hadn't noticed before. We see where God is working.

Much of the missional church literature encourages congregations and their leaders to notice where God is already at work in order to join in. Congregational vitality is sapped when good people start good projects, but something significant proves to be missing. The project never gets enough momentum, or volunteers drop out too soon.

Story after story in the missional church literature high-lights a pattern of people waiting until they perceive where God is already at work and what God is guiding them to do. When a group of Christians has discerned God's guid-ance, projects turn into exciting movements of God's Spirit that engage the congregation members as well as people in the wider community. Energy and enthusiasm grow. Cor-porate prayers of thankfulness can play a role in the kind of discernment that leads to vibrant ministries.

The kinds of thankfulness prayers that contribute to congregational discernment include paying attention to the source and direction of energy among people in the congre-gation, as well as the patterns of community life beyond the congregation. Where in the congregation and in the wider community are members serving with passion and imagi-nation? What needs in the wider community are already being met? By whom? In what ways? Where is the energy for service among members of the wider community?

Spending time thanking God for those patterns can help leaders or congregation members decide whether they are being called to join something already happen-ing or to start something new where God is beginning to work. Without taking the time to notice what God is already doing, congregations risk missing the pattern of what is arising in their midst, which makes mistakes more likely.

Prayers of thankfulness contribute to congregational discernment in other ways as well. Giving thanks reminds us—humans who often take ourselves and our efforts too seriously—that all ministry comes from God and is empowered by God. This lightens up any discernment process, enabling us to rest in God's guidance and power rather than straining for our own solution. And thankful-ness prayers remind us that God is working far beyond our homes and our churches. God is present in the lives of all people in one way or another, and thankfulness prayers encourage us to notice.

Thankfulness prayers also prod us to move beyond a simplistic view of how God answers prayer. In any time of discernment, when tentative steps are taken to begin a ministry in order to test whether this is the right direction and when many prayers are being offered for the success of the ministry, most groups of people will have preconceived ideas of what God's answers to prayer might look like. Pausing to thank God for anything and everything good that is occurring enables a group to perceive that God might be present in an unexpected way.

The Old Testament prophet Jeremiah notes that forgetting God can result in losing sight of the right road (15:15). His words are relevant to the role of thankfulness in discernment. In order to discern what God is doing *here*, in this specific church community and in the wider community around the church, we can't forget God. We need to remember the mighty acts of God in creation and redemption, and we also need to pay attention to the Spirit's work, in this place and in this community, providing for our needs and the needs of others, building relationships between unlikely people, performing small miracles, and answering prayer. All of these acts are part of the discernment process.

Fasting

In chapter 3 we saw that throughout Christian history fasting has been associated with asking for and receiving guidance from God. Acts 13:1–4 recounts an incident at Antioch when the Christians were worshiping and fasting as a group. The Holy Spirit spoke to them, saying, "Set apart for me Barnabas and Saul for the work to which I have called them" (v. 2). The group of Christians fasted and prayed for Barnabas and Saul (Paul) and sent them off.

Most Christians have heard numerous sermons about the ministry of Paul and Barnabas. If my own experience is any guide, very few of those sermons discuss the role of fasting in the calling of the two men. Yet people who fast talk about the way that fasting enables them to listen to God in new and fresh ways. Many Christians find that they are more open to God's guidance when fasting.

Often the process goes like this: A group of people decides to fast together in order to pray for specific prayer requests. Those requests might include asking God for guidance, or they might involve prayers for healing, jobs, or other needs. The group might fast from all foods, certain foods, or from something other than food, or individuals in the group might fast in different ways, but the fast centers on intercessory prayer empowered by fasting. The fast might go on for a day or a week or two, or even longer, and the people gather for communal prayer often during the fast.

As the fast progresses, the members of the group often find that their prayers shift in direction. They discover new ways to pray for the same things, or realize that new things to pray for are coming to mind. These shifts in prayer might happen when they are praying alone or when they pray as a group. Because they are fasting as a group, and because they are meeting together with some regularity during the fast, they are able to check their perceptions with each other: "I think God is leading me to pray this way rather than that way. What do you think? What are you sensing from God as you pray?"

Fasting contributes to the awareness that prayer is a dialogue with God rather than a monologue in which we tell God item after item that we're concerned about. Fasting helps us perceive the way that God wants us to pray about things. Because fasting helps us pray more closely in alignment with God's will, we are more able to discern what God is doing in a situation and what God might be calling us to do in response.

Contemplative Prayer
When we engage in contemplative prayer, we are trying to rest in God, dialogue with God, and learn from God.

Contemplative prayer primes our hearts to be available to God and to align our priorities with God's. These are valuable perspectives in a process of discernment.

The prayer of *examen* can play a part in a discernment process at any stage: beginning, middle, or end. The two questions in the prayer of *examen*—where was God in my life and where did I resist God's presence in my life?—are also key questions in a discernment process, because discernment involves observing the pattern of God's actions. At the beginning of a discernment process, these questions can set the stage and engage people with a process that affirms that we aren't running the show here, but we are trying to allow God to guide. At any point in the discernment process, these two questions can help restore the central focus of discernment. Even near the end, God's presence and our resistance to that presence are key issues. That's because discernment requires follow-up action, and action requires a continual focus on the fact that all ministry comes from God through Christ, empowered by the Spirit.

> *Just as the contemplative life has its roots . . . in the love of God, so too it overflows into acts of charity in the form of teaching, preaching and acts of mercy.*
>
> —Thomas S. Hibbs, "Wisdom Transformed by Love"

Centering prayer can also play a part in any stage of the discernment process; it can reduce tension and help a group to realign its focus onto God's will. Centering prayer, as its name implies, helps us find, over and over, God at the center of what we're doing and why we're doing it. In addition, we are more able to discern God's voice when we clear the clutter of other voices.

Examen, centering prayer, guided meditations, breath prayer, journaling, walking the labyrinth, and fixed-hour prayer can help participants learn to listen to God. People who engage in contemplative prayer grow in confidence that God does speak and that they can improve their ability to listen. Retreats are common settings for contemplative prayer, because being away from normal, everyday life can help us slow down, remove distractions, and focus on God. Retreats often play a role in discernment, because being away from the physical location of ministry can give us a fresh perspective on it. At retreats, contemplative prayer in any of its forms can smooth and empower the process of discernment.

Contemplative Approaches to Scripture

Lectio divina and Ignatian Gospel Contemplation (IGC) enable groups of people to encounter God through the Scriptures directly and with honesty. These two approaches to Scripture can help groups get beyond adversarial positions about specific issues because they can open up discussion into new areas. They can be helpful in a discernment process because they put everyone on an even playing field. No one is the expert, and one person is no more likely to hear God's voice through the Scripture than another.

These two prayerful ways of engaging with the Bible remind us that God is the one speaking and guiding us into ministry. In a discernment process, they need to be honored not only as a means to an end—making a decision about something—but as a way to hear God speak in a fresh way about something we may not even have been considering.

> *The major determinant of prayer or lectio is our fidelity to seeking God in everyday behavior. It is no good being fervent in reading if we are slack in living.*
>
> —Michael Casey, *Sacred Reading*

I vividly remember engaging in *lectio divina* at a session retreat more than a decade ago. The passage was about the dry bones in Ezekiel 37, and I still remember the impact of meditating on the wind that brought life to those bones. In my prayers in the past decade, I often return to the powerful pictures impressed on my mind during that *lectio divina* experience.

At that retreat, we interacted with Ezekiel 37 silently, for about twenty minutes, using the four stages of *lectio* that were printed for us on a sheet. After we had silently engaged with the passage, the leader invited us to share what we had experienced. We then went on to discuss the strategic planning issues that had been chosen as topics for the retreat.

It would have been inappropriate for the leader of the *lectio* to instruct us to focus on our own congregation's issues as we began the *lectio*. In this way of engaging with Scripture, the Holy Spirit needs to be allowed to speak about anything and everything, so the instructions for *lectio* always need to be open and broad, even in a time of discernment. However, when the *lectio* was finished, and after we had shared the ways God had spoken to us through the passage, the leader could have asked a few additional discussion questions rather than diving right into business, questions like these:

— Did you hear anything from God during the *lectio* that might help us as a leadership group?
— Did you sense God's direction for our congregation in any way?
— Did you perceive God's heart for our congregation in any new ways?

The Ezekiel passage might have led to some more specific questions as well:

— Did you hear something from God about any of the dry bones in our congregational life that God wants to bring to life?

— Did you perceive anything about the way God wants to blow wind over our congregation?

— When you think of God breathing life into our congregation, where do you see that happening?

Lectio divina and Ignatian Gospel Contemplation must not be viewed merely as techniques for hearing God speak about a congregation and its goals and strategies, although God may sometimes speak exactly that way. These contemplative approaches to Scripture, at any stage of a discernment process, need to remain open to God communicating about anything at all. However, if we have been seriously praying for God's guidance for our congregation, then we can expect that, at least from time to time, the Holy Spirit will speak to us about the questions we're asking, and some of that speaking may come from pondering God's Word.[1]

Hospitality

Of all the spiritual practices discussed in this book, it may seem that hospitality would be the least relevant to a process of discernment. After all, hospitality involves food preparation and washing dishes, very down-to-earth concerns. Hospitality requires welcoming people, with all their oddities and particular needs. It's a spiritual practice grounded in the here and now with all the attendant practical issues that surround any group of people.

But that "here and now" aspect of hospitality and the encounter with people are precisely why hospitality can play a significant role in congregational discernment. Part of the challenge of ministry today is figuring out exactly where and how God is calling us to serve the wider community. Listening to people's real needs and concerns, while comfortably eating a meal or having coffee together, helps us understand what's going on in the communities around us. The equality created by true hospitality removes the "we-they" mentality that so often makes community ministry uncomfortable for everyone concerned. Over spaghetti and garlic bread or coffee and brownies, stories are more honest. Needs and humor mingle in the conversation.

Hospitality in the midst of a discernment process might involve taking a break from prayer and discussion to eat together. It might involve inviting groups of people to sit at table, people who are stakeholders in the issues involved. It might include some meals or discussions over banana bread for congregation members and people in the wider community. The long history of breaking bread together as a way to create bonds between people is just as relevant in a discernment process as it is in any other setting.

> *Hospitality, rather than being something you achieve, is something you enter. . . . You make room for one person at a time, and each of these choices of the heart stretches your ability to receive others.*
>
> —Daniel Holman and Lonni Collins Pratt, *Radical Hospitality*

Ironically, both hospitality and fasting—eating and not eating, celebrating and abstaining—can play a role in a discernment process. Neither should be heralded as the one strategy that makes discernment work. Both are appropriate at the right time, and both may be unhelpful at other times. In fact, none of the spiritual disciplines described in this book should be viewed as the one key practice for discernment. A cluster of practices is more likely to be helpful, rather than focusing on just one.

Sabbath

My favorite Sabbath prayer comes from the Jewish tradition: "Days pass, years vanish, and we walk sightless among miracles."[2] Our sightlessness comes in part because we are so busy that we simply don't take the time to notice what God is doing around us. Our blindness also results from the value that we place on activity over reflection. In order to perceive where God might be calling us, we need to be able to see the miracles—large and small—that God is already doing. The practice of thankfulness encourages this kind of noticing. A Sabbath practice can also help us perceive the hand of God in our lives.

The Sabbath slows us down and makes time to step away from productivity. Long-term Sabbath observers emphasize that the Sabbath is about stopping, not about setting up new, and presumably more spiritual, things to do. The role of the Sabbath in congregational discernment does not come from hours on the Sabbath day spent in prayer, journaling, or other consciously reflective activities. The Sabbath gives space and freedom, which restore our perspective as beloved and dependent children of God. This grace-filled perspective is a key starting point for discernment, removing some of the tension and pressure that groups of Christians can feel as they seriously try to discern God's guidance.

When we get a glimpse, deep in our hearts, that we are beloved as we are, then our ego-driven need to prove our own worth diminishes. We can step aside from our idolatry of our own competence, energy, and actions. So much conflict in church leadership comes from the ego-based needs of the people involved, so the role of the Sabbath in imparting grace goes a long way to smooth the leadership process and soothe the people involved.

A Sabbath practice spills over into other moments of life. When people become used to stopping activity one day each week it becomes easier to engage in restful moments during the week, perhaps while sitting in a car at a stop light, standing in line at the bank, or sitting in

> *To choose to keep the Sabbath will irrevocably transform how we relate to the rest of the world.*
>
> —Marva J. Dawn, *Keeping the Sabbath Wholly*

a meeting where passionate and intense conversation has been swirling around. Those Sabbath moments during the week become opportunities for reflection.

Time for reflection is required when congregational leaders or members are asked to consider questions like, "Where do you think God's heart is for our congregation? Where do you think God is leading our congregation?" Without a practice of stopping productivity, those moments for reflection are few and far between. The Sabbath teaches stopping, a necessary skill for engaging in the kind of prayer and reflection that makes discernment possible.

Radical Discernment

All the spiritual disciplines mentioned above help keep the discernment process focused on the Triune God. This God in three persons created all things, and when we take time to notice God's creation, the way it was made and the way God sustains it, we remember who God is. Thankfulness, Sabbath keeping, contemplative prayer, and many other spiritual practices can help us remain attuned to our creator God.

God, the One who redeemed us in Jesus Christ, works to restore the brokenness in the world. Every time we notice an answer to prayer, every time we engage in hospitable acts that welcome people and their real stories into our lives, we are remembering Jesus our Redeemer. The Holy Spirit is the one who speaks God's truth to us, enables us to hear God's voice, and empowers us to obey God. Through the Spirit's power, these practices can help us follow God more nearly.

In fact, the process of discernment, which engages us with the Triune God, may be something almost incomprehensible to people who do not know God. Martin B. Copenhaver, a minister who led his congregation through a lengthy discernment process, reflected on the experience:

Spiritual discernment, rightly understood, is truly countercultural. It uses silence, it requires that we take our time, it redefines our precious sense of individualism. One other implication of spiritual discernment is a potential redistribution of power. If you must listen to each person with attentiveness because you never know who the Holy Spirit will choose to speak through at any given moment, then we must listen with as much care to a stranger as to a longstanding church member, we must listen as attentively to a young person as to a mature adult.[3]

Copenhaver observed that the practice of discernment allows participants to leave meetings energized and inspired, rather than discouraged and exhausted, and results in a renewed sense of who and what the church is called to be. The communal spiritual practices described in this book, along with others—including intercessory prayer, communal worship, singing, and Holy Communion—can lay a foundation for discernment and facilitate the flow of listening to each other and to God.

Spiritual practices, as a part of a discernment process, help individuals and groups listen for answers from God that address specific concerns and problems. Spiritual practices also help individuals and groups listen for and respond to God's direction into new priorities, fresh visions, and inventive ways to reflect God's love in the world.

Questions for Reflection, Discussion, or Journaling

1. When you think of God's guidance to you personally, in what settings and by what means do you most often experience it? When you think of God's guidance to the groups of people to which you belong, how does that guidance happen? What helps make the Holy Spirit's

voice more clear and vivid in the groups you have experienced? What do you think has made the Holy Spirit's guidance less clear?

2. Have your greatest obstacles to hearing God's voice come from an inability to listen or an unwillingness to obey? What patterns do you observe that contribute to your answer to that question? What might change those patterns?

3. In the groups in which you participate, have any of the six practices described in this chapter played a role in discernment? If so, what have been the benefits? The frustrations?

4. Can you imagine any of the six practices in this chapter playing a greater role in discernment in the groups in which you participate? What would be the obstacles? What might be the benefits? What would it take to introduce any of these six practices into your groups?

For Further Reading

Fendall, Lon, Jan Wood, and Bruce Bishop. *Practicing Discernment Together: Finding God's Way Forward in Decision Making.* Newberg, OR: Barclay Press, 2007. These Quaker authors describe the process of listening carefully to group members and also to the Holy Spirit working through them.

Morris, Danny E. and Charles M. Olsen. *Discerning God's Will Together: A Spiritual Practice for the Church.* Bethesda, MD: Alban Publications, 1997. This practical book provides many concrete steps that make congregational discernment possible.

9

ARE SPIRITUAL PRACTICES LEGALISTIC? ARE THEY A FORM OF SELF-HELP?

For freedom Christ has set us free. Stand firm, therefore, and do not submit again to a yoke of slavery.
—Galatians 5:1

William Willimon has launched an attack on the growing emphasis on spiritual practices. Willimon is a formidable advocate for his position. Formerly the dean of the chapel at Duke University and currently a United Methodist bishop in Alabama, he is one of the writers most frequently read by Protestant ministers in the United States.

In a 2010 article in the magazine *Christian Century*, Willimon writes:

My worry is that attention to practices deflects our attention from the living God. With the focus on practices, Christianity quietly morphs into a species of unbelief; we take revelation into our own hands. . . . The idea that we must do something for God before God will do anything for us, the concept that my relationship with God is sustained by my actions or feelings or inclinations, the notion that "religion" is something I do rather than God's effect on me — all these ideas appear to be lurking behind the contemporary discussions of practice.[1]

I heard the same concern from a student. In a casual conversation he told me, "There's so much rhetoric about spiritual practices — the idea seems to be that if I get the practice right, then I'll work my way to God." He went on to say that theologians throughout the ages have affirmed that God meets us. He argued that it is not our responsibility to engineer a meeting with God; in fact, it is impossible for us to do so.

If we are to advocate engaging in spiritual practices in our small groups and congregations, then we must think clearly and theologically about the ways spiritual practices contribute to Christian life, and we must be very certain that we are not engaging in self-help or trying to work our way to God. In this chapter I will begin by laying out William Willimon's arguments, and respond with my reflections on the significance of spiritual disciplines.

The Arguments against Spiritual Practice

In their landmark book, *Resident Aliens*, and in its sequel, *Where Resident Aliens Live*,[2] William Willimon and Stanley Hauerwas present a powerful and radical way of looking at Christian communal life, using images from the Old Testament about aliens who are resident in a community. In his 2010 *Christian Century* article, Willimon describes the central argument of *Resident Aliens*: "that Christianity is a communal tradition that gives us the skills, habits and practices that enable us truthfully to know the world in the way of Christ, and subversively to resist the toxic pressures of the world's godlessness."[3] The sequel, he notes, had the subtitle *Exercises for Christian Practice,* and encouraged the development of practices that would sustain and even transform Christians. In the *Christian Century* article, Willimon expresses regret for the strong emphasis he and his coauthor placed on Christian practices in the two books.

Willimon believes that the many books on Christian spiritual practices extol the virtues of those practices quite apart from God. In fact, he notes, an emphasis on practices can provide a way to avoid talking about God and to defend ourselves against God's unexpected and disconcerting interruptions into our lives. We know God and experience God's presence only as a gift from God, always as revelation, not primarily because of what we do. He believes the emphasis today on spiritual practices stands in a long line of attempts to live life on our terms.

In the article, Willimon notes that John Wesley, who strongly emphasized Christian practices, feared that Methodism could easily become a dead sect, "having the form of religion without the power."[4] Wesley believed this could happen if Methodists ceased to hold fast to doctrine and spirit, as well as discipline. The doctrines that Willimon stresses relate to God as "the wild, untamable Word . . . the true and living God who loves to meet people through the Word."[5]

> *In the spiritual life, discipline means to create that space in which something can happen that you hadn't planned or counted on.*
>
> —Henri Nouwen, "Moving from Solitude to Community to Ministry"

The *Christian Century* article in which Willimon expressed these opinions was reprinted in a slightly expanded version in a delightful collection of essays titled

A Spiritual Life, edited by Allan Hugh Cole, Jr.[6] In the expanded version, Willimon makes two additional points. He wonders if spiritual practices may be the latest phase in functional atheism. God often feels absent, and we don't like that feeling. He suggests that perhaps we engage in spiritual practices as one more way of helping us feel better about these feelings of God's absence. God seems to be hidden from us, and we seek to alleviate the discomfort of that seeming reality by doing *something*.[7]

Willimon also describes an interaction with a Hindu student that occurred when he was the dean of the chapel at Duke. This student complained about the way a professor talked about Hinduism in a course on world religions. The professor, the student said, described Hinduism as a set of rather dull ideas, while in reality Hinduism entails a complex set of practices—even involving smells—which are virtually incomprehensible to outsiders.[8]

I have had similar conversations about Hinduism and other religions in my department. For the past five years, I have been teaching in a "theology and religion" department in a university where Christian theology, biblical studies, and church history are taught alongside courses on many of the world's religions. To my shame, before I joined this department I knew very little about the religions of the world beyond the Abrahamic traditions of Christianity, Judaism, and Islam. Because Christianity has creeds in which we affirm what we believe, I assumed most other religions had at least some creedal elements. I have come to understand that many religions are self-defined more by practices than by belief systems. Christians may have the tendency to seek to understand the belief systems of other religions. However, we might be better off examining the practices associated with those religions. Might the same be true to some extent as we look at Christian communities? Are the practices associated with our faith indicators of something significant about the outworking of what we believe?

Departmental seminars, reading groups, and conversations with my colleagues have stimulated my thinking about the role of practices in various religions, and thus also the role of practices in Christian life. Willimon's article came at a good time for me, continuing my reflection on this question. I agree with Willimon that none of our actions earn us God's approval or love. This God, whom we worship and serve, loves us beyond all comprehension. In Christ, this God breaks into human life. Through the Holy Spirit, this God speaks to us, encounters us, shapes us, and empowers us. We cannot make the Holy Spirit do anything.

God is amazing, and yes, God is untamable and wild, as Willimon suggested. We should never stop being open to unexpected encounters with this amazing God. In fact, God is always the initiator. God reaches out to us as our Creator, as our Redeemer in Jesus Christ, and as our Sustainer through the Holy Spirit. Therefore, any action we take as an attempt to draw near to God has to be viewed as a response to the initiative God has already taken.

> *Salvation is being engrafted into practices that save us from those powers that would rule our lives making it impossible for us to truly worship God.*
>
> —Stanley Hauerwas,
> *In Good Company*

And yet I still affirm that Christian practices have great significance in enabling us to hear God's wild, untamable Word to us so that we can grow into the image and likeness of Jesus. I believe spiritual practices make space for us to encounter and hear this God who is already with us and in us and speaking to us. Spiritual disciplines—with the emphasis on the word discipline—help us to embrace the structures and habits that shape our characters more into the image of Christ. Spiritual disciplines are a means by which we respond to God's call, and they in turn open us to God's further action in our lives.

Our Relationship with God

If I had to say what I believe Christianity is, what it means to follow Jesus, I wouldn't explain it as primarily a practice or a set of beliefs to which I give assent, although both practices and beliefs play a significant role. I view being a Christian primarily as a relationship with God, a friendship with Jesus (John 15:12–17) through the power of the Holy Spirit, in which we are invited into the loving and self-giving relationship among the three persons of the Trinity. The triune God lives in love, and welcomes us into that love, encouraging us to draw near and even participate in this communal life.

The language Jesus uses in John 15 about our invitation into friendship with him evokes a picture of Jesus walking beside us on the road or Jesus' presence with us in every life situation. Spiritual practices, as Adele Ahlberg Calhoun notes, help us to "keep company with Jesus."[9] When we pray alone or in a group, when we fast, and when we keep the Sabbath with the desire to keep company with Jesus, we are not inviting Jesus to come and walk with us. Instead, we are opening ourselves to experience Jesus' presence. Jesus is *already* beside us and with us, even if we often can't hear his voice because we are so busy or preoccupied.

Willimon does acknowledge the significance of some spiritual disciplines, at least for preachers: "The spiritual practices needed by faithful Christian preachers are those that give us the guts to be in conversation with, and to speak up for, a true and living God who loves to meet people through the Word."[10] Friendship includes a strong component of listening, and Jesus' invitation into friendship with him must, by definition, include a lot of conversation and listening. Many Christian spiritual disciplines facilitate listening to God, so the priority Willimon places on conversation is addressed in those spiritual practices.

Spiritual disciplines, as a way to make ourselves available to God, address the priority Willimon places on having the guts to "speak up for" this "true and living God who loves to meet people through the Word." At the beginning of chapter 4, when I introduced contemplative prayer, I spoke about the "aha" moment when I realized that contemplative prayer was making me more available to God, and how right and good that was. Richard Foster and Gayle Beebe, in *Longing for God*, use slightly different language to make the same point:

> Prayer is not telling God what we think, or simply thanking him for his provision of food and drink. Rather it is our active, intentional effort to understand what God is doing and how we can join him. Thus through prayer we become coparticipants with God. God's will sets everything in motion. Our will, directed by devotion and prayer, allows us to participate in his purposes. Together, prayer and devotion form our inner being.[11]

I can imagine that William Willimon might object to some of the language that Foster and Beebe use. He might ask whether we, through our actions, can become coparticipants with God. Is it not God, through the Holy Spirit, who enables us to participate in serving the world? Yes, only the Holy Spirit can make us coparticipants, but saints and wise Christians through the ages have affirmed that our "active, intentional efforts to understand what God is doing and how we can join him"[12] do make a difference. Only the Holy Spirit can make us coparticipants with God, but we have to be willing to let that participation happen. Spiritual disciplines are one way we express our willingness to learn of God's ways and participate in fulfilling God's desires for the world. And the spiritual disciplines themselves are acts of coparticipation. These acts make a difference, even as we affirm that God initiates and provides power for all of them.

Our availability to God and our willingness to be coparticipants with God can be an aspect of the friendship with God that Jesus speaks about. When we have a good friend, we enter into the priorities of that friend, and we long to be a part of what our friend cares about. We want to help friends, and we partner with them as they do things. Jesus says that he doesn't call his disciples "servants" any longer, "because the servant does not know what the master is doing; but I have called you friends, because I have made known to you everything that I have heard from my Father" (John 15:15). As Jesus makes known to us the priorities and goals of the Triune God, we will hopefully grow in having the guts to speak up for this God, as Willimon advocates. But first, in order to know the purposes and priorities of a friend, and in order to know how to speak boldly in a way that reflects what our friend cares about, we need to spend time together and to listen. Spiritual practices open up time with Jesus and enable listening.

> *O God, the Triune God, I want to want Thee; I long to be filled with longing; I thirst to be made more thirsty still.*
>
> —A. W. Tozer,
> *The Pursuit of God*

This picture of friendship with Jesus and the invitation into the triune life of God through that friendship is only one way of looking at what it means to be a Christian. Jesus not only stands beside us as a friend; Jesus also lives in us. In Colossians, the Apostle Paul speaks of the mystery hidden throughout the ages but now revealed: "Christ in you, the hope of glory" (1:27).

Christ is in us, and we are in Christ. Many of the New Testament epistles begin with a greeting to the "saints in Christ Jesus" (for example, Philippians 1:1), and 1 Peter ends with this blessing: "Peace to all of you who are in

Christ" (5:14). And one of the most often quoted statements in the New Testament includes this same idea: "If anyone is in Christ, there is a new creation" (2 Cor. 5:17). These passages indicate that we are in Christ both as individuals and as a community.

We are in Christ, and Christ is in us. Spiritual practices can make this reality clear and evident. So many spiritual practices involve abiding or resting in God, and slowing down long enough to pay attention to the reality of our life in Christ and Christ's life in us. Contemplative prayer, contemplative approaches to Scripture, Sabbath keeping, and fasting all have strong components of waiting on God, resting in God, and allowing God to be God in our lives. When spiritual practices become a way to prove that we are spiritually profound or to earn God's approval, we are violating the essence of New Testament faith, which emphasizes this presence of God in us and beside us, at God's initiative and through the power of the Holy Spirit.

The Work of the Holy Spirit

Another lens for viewing spiritual disciplines comes from considering the work of the Holy Spirit. The Holy Spirit teaches us Jesus' priorities and values (John 14:26 and 16:8–13), nudging us to see what Jesus views as true and right and good, and also giving us the strength to follow what we see. Through the work of the Holy Spirit in us, we are invited into the truth about the way the universe works, as seen through the eyes of the One who created it. We are invited to participate in the ongoing work of redemption in this broken world.

In order to see God's priorities and engage with them, we need to be transformed. I see spiritual practices as vitally necessary for this transformation. Yes, we are new creatures because we are in Christ, but we still need ongoing transformation. As anyone knows who has struggled with anger, bad habits, or vicious thoughts long after becoming a Christian, the new creation in Christ needs continual shaping. The New Testament affirms a life-long process of growing into the image of Christ. All of us, the Apostle Paul writes, "seeing the glory of the Lord as though reflected in a mirror, are being transformed into the same image from one degree of glory to another; for this comes from the Lord, the Spirit" (2 Cor. 3:18).

> *The goal of Christian spirituality is to be enlivened by God's Spirit.*
>
> —Tony Jones, *The Sacred Way*

In this passage, the emphasis is on transformation into the image of Christ through the work of the Holy Spirit. And yet we have a role in this transformation as well. "Do not be conformed to this world, but be transformed by the renewing of your minds, so that you may discern what is the will of God—what is good and acceptable and perfect" (Rom. 12:2). This verse in Romans stands as a useful partner to the verse in 2 Corinthians. The Holy Spirit transforms us, but we participate by choosing not to be conformed to the world and by renewing our minds. Our actions and thoughts matter.

Spiritual practices are one way that Christians throughout the ages have participated in being transformed into the image of Christ. I have said that spiritual practices open up time with Jesus and enable listening. These contribute to the Holy Spirit's work of transformation in us, so spiritual practices can be intentional actions to help us grow into the image of Christ. But spiritual practices are also simply descriptions of what sanctified human life looks like when God gets hold of our human flesh and our human spirits. We become more like Jesus because of the work of the Spirit in us.

All habitual actions shape us. The more we yell at our kids, the more we grow accustomed to yelling at them. The more often we take out the garbage, the more we become used to a sweet-smelling kitchen and the more motivated we are to continue to take the garbage out frequently. The more we look for things for which to express thanks to God, the more blessings and gifts from God we will see. The more we meditate on the Bible, the easier it will become to spend long periods of time with the Scriptures.

One of the most helpful aspects of Willimon's warnings about spiritual practices relates to the way habits transform us. He is right to say that if we are looking for practices to shape us into the image of Christ apart from the work of the Holy Spirit, we are engaging in unbelief. This form of unbelief involves taking religion into our own hands, behaving as if our relationship with God is nurtured by our own efforts and Christian life is something we do on our own rather than allowing God to work in us. We must realize that God works in us to transform us and that spiritual practices indicate our willingness for that to happen or reveal the ways that it is happening through the work of the Holy Spirit in us.

Another helpful aspect of Willimon's perspective comes from his emphasis on God's pattern of unexpected and disconcerting interruptions, attested to by saints throughout the ages. If we try to control the experience we have when we engage in spiritual practices, then we shut out the God of the unexpected. Most people who have invested significant time in spiritual practices talk about the ways God surprises them. People who participate in *lectio divina* talk about the unexpected emphases they hear from God as they meditate on the Bible. People who fast articulate the shifts in prayer that so often happen during a fast. They start off with a specific prayer request, but by the end of the fast God has nudged them to pray for that request in a different way, or to pray for something else entirely. People who practice intentional hospitality are always surprised by the way God meets them in extraordinary ways through unexpected people.

If part of the purpose of spiritual practices is to keep company with Jesus and to abide in our untamable, disconcerting

God, then we can expect to experience surprises. The possibility of surprises needs to be included when we teach about spiritual disciplines and the way practices function in the Christian life. These are not random and meaningless surprises. They come from the wild God who meets us in Jesus Christ through the radical power of the Holy Spirit, the God who initiates all connection between humans and God. These surprises are part of the work of transformation that the Holy Spirit does in us. Surprises remind us, deep in our hearts, that God is God and we are not.

John Wesley was concerned about spiritual practices that would perpetuate stale religion without power. An emphasis on true openness to God and willingness to be surprised can go a long way to reducing the possibility that powerless religion will happen. A commitment to cooperate in transformation into Christ's image, empowered by the Holy Spirit, keeps spiritual disciplines alive and fresh, rather than dull attempts to prove our worth to God.

Becoming like Jesus

If Christ is in us and we are in Christ, then we can expect that we will become more like Jesus. And of course Jesus engaged in spiritual practices. Jesus' first public appearance took place in the synagogue during the Sabbath, when he read from the scroll of the prophet Isaiah (Luke 4:16–21), and Jesus kept the Sabbath even as he reframed the discipline's priorities by performing miracles on the Sabbath. Jesus fasted (Luke 4:1–13) and spent time alone in prayer (Mark 1:35). And when he prayed, he expressed his submission to the will of his Father (Luke 22:39–42 and John 17). Jesus is our model for engaging in spiritual practices.

Jesus also instructs his disciples about the spiritual practices of gathering together and the Lord's Supper (Matt. 18:20 and Luke 22:19–20). When Christians gather for worship and partake communion together, they are engaging in the central communal practices of the people of God. Over time, corporate worship and the sacraments can shape us more into the likeness of Jesus. Many books rightly discuss the significance of communal worship and the sacraments for the Christian life. This book focuses on other communal practices that have not received as much attention.

The practices of the Christian life—including corporate worship and the sacraments, and also other practices—play a role in the Holy Spirit's work of helping us become more like Jesus. The consistent practice of thankfulness helps us identify more easily the way God is working in the world, opening our eyes and giving us better vision like Jesus had. Fasting enables us to hear God's voice leading us in prayer, and can prompt us to confess our sins. Contemplative prayer encourages us to grow in our availability to God and our experience of God's peace. Contemplative approaches to Scripture hone the skill of listening to the voice of the Holy Spirit through the Word of God. Hospitality gives us humility and the ability to hear the voice of God through the people created by and loved by God. The Sabbath moves many biblical truths from our head to our heart, helping us know more deeply that we are beloved creatures of a wildly extravagant God, and the Sabbath causes us to slow down long enough to observe God's presence in our lives. Jesus manifested these actions and characteristics, and spiritual disciplines help us experience them and persevere in them.

Spiritual disciplines can help us find a balance point between two extremes that are all too common in individual and congregational spirituality today. At one end of the spectrum is a magical view that leaves everything in God's hands as if God were a magician, making things happen totally apart from us. This magical view of God makes Christians lazy. Why should we put a load of work into covering all our bases when we apply for the permit to expand our church building? God will either make it happen or not. Why should we carefully analyze our congregational communication when the Holy Spirit is the one who really does the communication in our congregation anyway?

At the other end of the spectrum is the "management" view of Christian spirituality and congregational life, which affirms that our planning, organization, and attention to detail make everything happen. When we're functioning with a management view, we affirm a set of beliefs about God, but we don't expect God to be actively present among us.

> *[God] cannot be found by any work of your soul, but only by the love of your heart.*
>
> — *The Cloud of Unknowing*

Christian spiritual disciplines, when exercised faithfully and biblically, attest to the action of God as well as the responsibility of humans. Christian practices hold both extremes in tension rather than overemphasizing one or the other. One of my early mentors compared the Christian life to a piece of music in 2/4 time. The downbeat of each measure is the action of God, and the second beat is our response. God always initiates, and we are always called to respond.

Allowing Grace to Shape Us

Spiritual practices provide one answer to a key question: what do we do after we receive grace in order to let grace shape us? Modernity has emphasized personal freedom, and we've seen both negative and positive results of that freedom. I'm free to eat all the cookies I want, but I easily become addicted to sugar, and my life has often been diminished by the way sugar tends to make me gain weight with amazing speed. Limiting the number of cookies I eat restricts my freedom in one sense, but it gives me a freedom not to struggle with my weight as much. Likewise, I have chosen to limit my activities on the Sabbath because I want to enjoy the freedom I have as a beloved child of God. Spiritual disciplines limit our freedom in one way, but they can open us up to grace, which gives us true freedom in Christ.

After *Christian Century* published the article by William Willimon about spiritual practices, the editors received letters in response, and they printed several of them in a later issue. Willimon, who received the chance to respond, said, "My modest point in the article was to say that Christian practices must be commensurate with the worship of and service to the trinitarian God."[13] Amen. Spiritual practices should be viewed as a part of Christian worship in which we give our lives to the Trinitarian God who has reached out to us in Christ. They are part of our response to the work of the Holy Spirit in us, and they are evidence of the Holy Spirit's transformation of our lives. They should not be embraced as ways to earn God's approval or make ourselves better people apart from God. They involve growing in our ability to keep company with Jesus and to stay open to the Holy Spirit, to experience true freedom in Christ.

One of the letters to the editor, in response to Willimon's article, noted that the tone of the message of the biblical story usually goes like this: "Here is what God has done . . . Because God has already done this, here is what you should do in response to the proactive God." This letter writer is describing the two-beat rhythm of the Christian life. Then he goes on to say, "Christian discipleship is an expression of gratitude, not theological bribery" and "Such practices are not in danger of diverting us from God, but rather are demonstrating to the world the heart of the God whom we serve."[14] I'll say Amen again.

Questions for Reflection, Discussion, or Journaling

1. Do you view the essence of following Jesus primarily as a relationship, a group of practices, or a set of beliefs to which you give assent? What do you think are the major forces in your life that have made this perspective

significant to you? What do you think are the pros and cons of your viewpoint?

2. Have you met God or heard God's voice in a surprising, unexpected way when you engaged in a spiritual practice, either individually or corporately? What emotions do you feel when you think about that incident? In what ways do you try to stay open to God's wild, untamable nature?

3. Have you experienced transformation through a spiritual practice that you have engaged in, either individually or corporately? In what ways has that spiritual practice made you more like Jesus? In what ways did the Holy Spirit work through your practice?

4. Have spiritual practices become a bit like self-help in your life? Do you ever fall into the trap of thinking that God might love you more because of something you do? What helps you return to a view that keeps God's grace at the center?

For Further Reading

Cole, Allan Hugh, Jr., editor. *A Spiritual Life*. Louisville, KY: Westminster John Knox Press, 2011. This fabulous book is full of stories by individuals who discuss what it means to view their lives as having a spiritual focus. The chapter by Willimon (an expanded version of the *Christian Century* article mentioned above) is unusual in the book because it presents didactic arguments rather than stories.

Yancey, Philip. *What's So Amazing About Grace?* Grand Rapids: Zondervan, 2002. Many people have told me that this book, more than any other, helped them learn to experience God's grace in everyday life.

10

RECEPTIVITY:
THE GIFT OF SPIRITUAL
PRACTICES

Lord, you have been our dwelling-place
in all generations.
Before the mountains were brought forth,
or ever you had formed the earth and the world,
from everlasting to everlasting you are God.
— Psalm 90:1–2

About ten years ago I led a worship service at a retreat.
The setting was intimate, unlike the Sunday worship services at church where the leader—sometimes me—usually stood some distance away from the congregation. At
the end of the retreat worship, I said a benediction. To my
surprise, several of the younger women sitting close to me
turned their hands so their palms faced up. They looked as
if they were trying to catch the benediction in their hands.

I had often said, "Now, receive the benediction" before I
ended a worship service, and these women looked as if they

were taking those words seriously. They used their hands to indicate a posture of the heart, a posture of receptivity.

What might they have been trying to receive? What might they have been longing for?

Perhaps some of them had a specific need in mind as they turned their hands up to "catch" God's blessing. Perhaps they were hoping for God's action related to a specific need in their families or in their jobs, or maybe they were hoping for God's guidance in a particular situation. Perhaps they had learned something new about God at the weekend retreat, and they were hoping God would cement that new knowledge into their lives. They could have had many other specific needs, requests, or situations on their minds as they used their hands to "receive" the benediction.

Perhaps some of them were simply open to more of God in their lives. Perhaps the motion of their hands expressed a willingness to receive anything and everything from God, an indication of their commitment to be disciples of Jesus who would follow their Master wherever he might lead them.

What Is Receptivity?

When I use this word "receptivity," I am referring to being open to God's gifts and God's guidance in two different ways. On the one hand, God works in our lives in response to the needs we express in prayer, the concerns we have about people we love, and the tensions and anxieties we experience in everyday life. God invites us to open our hearts and minds to see the way the Holy Spirit is moving in the situations we care about. Spiritual disciplines go a long way toward enabling us to see God's activity because they help us slow down, recognize patterns, and listen to God.

The second aspect of receptivity relates to our willingness to let God initiate, to let God be God in whatever form that takes. Jesus invites us to follow him, to let him set the agenda and lead us. "Take my yoke upon you and learn from me," Jesus encourages us (Matt. 11:29). God guides us into places we wouldn't otherwise go, and challenges us to grow in ways we never imagined. God gives us gifts that we could never have seen on our own, and calls us to use them in situations we never planned. Spiritual practices help us receive these utterly unexpected and unplanned moments of grace.

During the writing of this book I have been observing the moments in my daily life when I am receptive to God. Many begin with a specific need. *God, I need your help with this problem I'm having. Help me to be open to your guidance and your wisdom about this situation.* Less frequent are moments of receptivity where I express my willingness to go anywhere and do anything God asks of me. *I want to follow you, Jesus. Guide me today into the life you have for me, no matter how unexpected it might be. Help me to hear your voice. My life is yours, not my own.* These moments happen most often when I have heard a good sermon, received communion, read an inspiring portion of the Bible, fasted, spent time in contemplative prayer, walked a labyrinth, or prayed with a group of people. In other words, these moments happen most often when I have engaged in a spiritual practice that has opened my heart to the call of God into my life.

> *Patient receptivity may serve us better than a clamorous urgency to be enlightened.*
>
> —Michael Casey, *Sacred Reading*

I suspect that many readers of this book have similar patterns of receptivity — times of being open to God's guidance about troublesome aspects of life and other moments of willingness to do whatever God asks. This posture of receptivity, in both aspects, flows naturally from being a Christian and trying to live in obedience and service to God. We need help in nurturing such receptivity in our individual lives, and one task of congregations is to help equip members to live in an increasingly receptive attitude. Communal spiritual practices help us as individuals to develop the patterns that draw us near to God in an open, listening posture.

So often we come to God in prayer, or we think about God's work in our lives, with a specific agenda in mind. This is true of individuals and also of congregations. In our congregations we might be worried about one of the missionaries we support, so we pray for help for that missionary. The budget might be in trouble and we ask God to guide us in our response to this need. Or the youth director has announced that she got a new job, so we pray for her replacement. We express our openness to hear God's guidance in these specific situations. Those prayers are good and essential, but they focus only on the aspects of God's work in our lives that we are thinking about in any given moment. They come largely from our initiative, even though we couldn't have prayed them if God hadn't loved us first.

An attitude of receptivity encourages us to go one step beyond our immediate concerns and opens us to God's initiative in our midst in a new way. Perhaps God is calling our congregation to engage with the local elementary school, the neighborhood food bank, or the students at a local college. Will we hear God's guidance in that direction? Perhaps God is calling us to trust in new ways as we plan the budget or to reconsider that building renovation we have been debating for years. Will we listen? Spiritual practices encourage congregational leaders and members to expect that God will be speaking—and teach them to hear more clearly.

Why Receptivity Is Necessary Today

Numerous cultural shifts make this posture of receptivity more compelling for congregations today than it was in the second half of the twentieth century. In the past fifty years, the pattern of congregational life has changed dramatically. For many congregations in the United States and in other countries as well, the period after World War II was a time of abundance. Adults and children flooded into church buildings. Money was relatively easy to come by for congregational projects. For many families, one salary was enough to live on, so the nonworking spouse could volunteer in the Sunday school program, provide food for funerals and weddings, or help in the church office. Even many working people had enough leisure time to volunteer significant amounts of time at church.

The numerous changes in everyday life in the past six or seven decades have had a profound impact on congregations. Increased working hours and financial pressure mean that people have less energy, time, and money to contribute to their congregations. The increasingly secular culture pulls people away from the church. Some congregations, of course, did not experience abundance and ease in the mid-twentieth century, so they might not see a current dearth of money, time, or energy as anything new. However, other subtle shifts are affecting just about every congregation and necessitating a move toward greater receptivity in our congregational life. Some additional significant cultural shifts include:

Our multicultural society. Global migration has brought Buddhists, Hindus, and Muslims into many neighborhoods that used to be more homogeneous. As Christians encounter people who are faithful to other religions, many questions come up about our own spiritual practices and beliefs. Some of those questions can be addressed through engagement with spiritual practices, which bring life and energy to congregations and help make visible what exactly it means to be a Christian. Communal spiritual practices help congregations experience a real relationship with God in Jesus Christ through the power of the Holy Spirit, and they enable congregations to move into a posture of receptivity that involves listening to and responding to this Living God we worship. What are the unique contributions of the Christian faith in a pluralistic world? People who have had an experience of the living Word are able to give an answer.

The drive for authenticity. In the past few years, I've been hearing the word "authenticity" used by younger Christians—as well as some Christians my own age—to express what they long to find in their congregations. I recently read a blog post by a woman in her thirties, a mom with three kids. She expressed her frustration about so many church activities that seem no different than what might happen at a club or class. Her words capture the essence of what I've heard from many other individuals:

> **We are hungry for authenticity and vulnerability.**
> . . . Some of us are drowning, suffocating, dying of thirst for want of the cold water of real community. . . .
> **We need Jesus.** We are seeking deep spirituality. We are seeking fellow travelers. We are hungry for true community, a place to tell our stories and listen to [one] another, to love well. But above all, point me to Jesus—not to the sale at the mall. We want to change the world. . . . We want to give and serve and make a difference. We want to be challenged. . . . We want to listen to each other. We want to worship, we want to intercede for our sisters and weep with those who weep, rejoice with those that rejoice, to create life and art and justice with intention.[1]

Many of this blogger's longings can be facilitated by communal spiritual practices and the receptivity to the Living God that is nurtured through them.

An emphasis on personal experiences and needs. The consumer culture stresses personal needs, which spill over into personal spiritual needs. Like the woman quoted above, Christians today may be more in touch with their unique spiritual needs than earlier Christians were. I often decry a culture that overemphasizes personal needs, but I have to admit that accessing our personal, inner desire for God is a good thing. In addition, in many settings in the past few decades, personal experience has become more compelling than duty or responsibility. Many people who engage in spiritual practices like fasting, Sabbath keeping, hospitality, and various forms of contemplative experiences talk about the personal needs that are met through those practices. Such practices lead them toward experiencing the presence of God in new ways.

Spiritual Practices in Congregations

Developing a posture of receptivity involves much more than cupping our hands to receive a benediction at the end of a worship service. But that act of turning hands upside down to catch God's blessing can be a manifestation of a heart that wants, more than anything else, to receive from God.

Spiritual practices transform us and are also a sign of the coming kingdom, a foretaste of the pattern of life that we will experience in heaven, when intimacy with God will no longer be marred by human sin. When we participate in intentional spiritual practices, alone or with others, our lives are a bit more like the life of Jesus, the One into whose image we are being transformed.

We are whole and unified beings. Body, mind, and spirit work together and play a role in helping us draw nearer to the Triune God. Spiritual practices can help us come into God's presence with our whole beings. This wild and amazing God calls us into a love relationship and invites us to draw near with everything we are and everything we have. Spiritual practices as experienced in Christian community help us do that with joy and hope, and can help congregations prepare for a vibrant future.

Questions for Reflection, Discussion, or Journaling

1. Imagine yourself holding your hands open to God. What would you want to receive?

2. Spend some time pondering the pattern of your prayer life. In what ways and in what settings do you bring your own requests, your own agenda, to God in prayer? In what ways and in what settings are you open to God's agenda? What would you like to shift or change in your prayer priorities?
3. Think about the pattern of prayer and spiritual practices in your small group or your congregation. In what ways and settings do you experience a communal openness to what God is doing or wants to do, quite apart from the group's agenda? In what ways can you imagine your small group or congregation engaging in some of the practices described in this book? In what ways do you think those practices might nurture an attitude of communal receptivity to God?

For Further Reading

Brother Lawrence. *The Practice of the Presence of God.* (Numerous editions available.) This centuries-old classic, beloved by generations of Christians, gives a model for experiencing God's presence in the midst of daily life.

Ford, Leighton. *The Attentive Life: Discerning God's Presence in All Things.* Downers Grove, IL: InterVarsity Press, 2008. Filled with beautiful quotations and a deep sense of wonder at God's invitation to us to draw near, this book offers vivid descriptions of what attentiveness to God looks like in practice.

Foster, Richard J. *Celebrating the Disciplines: A Journal Workbook to Accompany* Celebration of Discipline. New York: HarperOne, 1992. This one-year workbook helps make the ideas in *Celebration of Discipline* more real and concrete. Useful for both individuals and groups.

APPENDIX

COMMUNICATING STRATEGICALLY ABOUT SPIRITUAL DISCIPLINES

*It is he [Jesus Christ] whom we proclaim, warning everyone
and teaching everyone in all wisdom, so that we may present
everyone mature in Christ.*
—Colossians 1:28

In congregations, people learn many things by osmosis and informal communication, and we must never discount the communication that goes on in networks of relationships. If a few individuals get very excited about something, the news will spread. These days news may spread through conversations, e-mail, text messages, Facebook posts, or blogs. If a congregational emphasis on spiritual disciplines takes off, the people in the congregation will undoubtedly contribute to the upsurge through informal communication, and this is a wonderful thing.

However, informal communication is usually spotty. Some people get left out. A congregational emphasis on spiritual disciplines requires intentional teaching and communication. The lists below can get you started thinking about where and how to communicate an increased commitment to spiritual practices.

In addition, many people are experiential learners. Spiritual disciplines particularly lend themselves to experiential learning, and sometimes offering an experience of a spiritual discipline is the best way to teach about it. The list below incorporates both information and action that can help nurture a focus on spiritual practices in congregations.

During Worship Services

— Offer prayers of thankfulness
— Experience *lectio divina* or Ignatian Gospel Contemplation
— Attempt breath prayer, a guided meditation, or *examen*
— Announce dates for spiritual practices to be done as a congregation such as fasts or hospitality events
— Announce training or teaching about spiritual disciplines
— Present resources for small groups

Small Groups or Adult Classes

— Work through a study guide related to spiritual disciplines
— Teach and experience contemplative prayer, *lectio divina*, or Ignatian Gospel Contemplation
— For Bible study groups, spend one week on the passage doing Bible study discussion and spend the second week on the same passage doing *lectio divina*
— For Bible studies of Gospel passages use Ignatian Gospel Contemplation with all the steps described in chapter 5

— Host hospitality events for each other and for friends and neighbors
— Keep a Sabbath together
— Share stories about Sabbath observance in childhood and the present
— Begin prayer times with prayers of thanksgiving
— Start a list of things your group is thankful for
— Plan a fast together

Sermons
— Explain spiritual disciplines in the Bible and their relevance for today
— Describe and explain specific spiritual disciplines
— Relate testimonies and stories about spiritual disciplines
— Mention helpful books on spiritual disciplines
— Engage in *lectio divina* or Ignatian Gospel Contemplation during sermon preparation
— Model Ignatian Gospel Contemplation by helping the congregation imagine they are participants in a Gospel story

Church Newsletter
— Offer brief articles describing practical issues related to spiritual disciplines
— Print members' testimonies about their experiences with spiritual disciplines
— Announce dates to begin and end engagement with specific disciplines
— Relay prayer requests for fasts
— Publicize dates and times for hospitality events
— Publicize dates and times for adult classes or book groups on spiritual disciplines
— Describe resources for small groups that focus on spiritual disciplines
— Review helpful books on spiritual disciplines

Church Web Site
— Post short and long articles describing practical issues related to spiritual disciplines
— Post members' testimonies about their experiences with spiritual disciplines
— Announce dates to begin and end engagement with specific disciplines
— Relay prayer requests for fasts
— Link to Scripture passages relevant to spiritual practices
— Link to resources that are available online
— Offer resources for small groups, either online or in printed form in booklets and books
— Review books
— Announce adult classes or book groups focused on spiritual disciplines

Minister's Blog or Congregational Blog
— Submit personal testimonies
— Review books, study guides, and curricula about spiritual disciplines
— Teach about spiritual disciplines
— Remind members of start and end dates for communal spiritual disciplines
— Describe things to be thankful for
— Link to online resources

Facebook and Twitter
— Post reminders of dates for classes, book groups, or the beginning or end of specific disciplines
— Post reminders of prayer requests
— Encourage brief testimonies
— Link to online resources
— Link to resources for small groups

As we saw in chapter one, Lent and Advent provide an excellent opportunity for congregational engagement with spiritual disciplines. These two seasons of the church year are finite in time, and historically they have been seasons of reflection and penitence. Any one of the spiritual practices described in this book, and many others as well, would be appropriate for a congregational emphasis during Lent or Advent.

I want to recommend two specific sources that have resources about spiritual disciplines for small groups and adult classes. First, The Thoughtful Christian (www .thethoughtfulchristian.com) provides lessons on a wide variety of topics, including spiritual practices. I've written several lessons for The Thoughtful Christian. I've also written several Bible study guides for InterVarsity Press, which has a good number of study guides focused on spiritual practices (www.ivpress.com).

NOTES

Chapter 1: Discipline? No Thanks!

1. Marjorie J. Thompson, *Soul Feast: An Invitation to the Christian Spiritual Life* (Louisville, KY: Westminster John Knox Press, 1995), xv.

2. Tony Jones, *The Sacred Way: Spiritual Practices for Everyday Life* (Grand Rapids: Zondervan, 2005), 30–31.

3. Adele Ahlberg Calhoun, *Spiritual Disciplines Handbook* (Downers Grove, IL: InterVarsity Press, 2005), 17.

4. Alan Roxburgh, *Missional Mapmaking: Skills for Leading in Times of Transition* (San Francisco: Jossey-Bass, 2010), 151–52.

5. Ibid., 152.

6. In November 2010, I had the privilege of hearing Alan Roxburgh lead a seminar on the missional church. He asked, "How do you take a bunch of Christians who have been socialized into a tradition and resocialize them into new habits? How do we invite them into asking the question, 'Where is God at work in this neighborhood and how can we join in?'"

Chapter 2: Thankfulness

1. Children are invited to participate in the candle lighting. Because the tray is on the stage, above the reach

of the youngest children, only older children are able to participate without help from their parents, which increases the safety of the experience. Younger children need their parents to help lift them up to reach the candles.

2. David Steindl-Rast, *Gratefulness, the Heart of Prayer* (New York: Paulist Press, 1984), 15–17.

3. Words by Martin Rinkart (1586–1649), translated by Catherine Winkworth (1827–1878), accessible online at http://www.cyberhymnal.org/htm/n/o/nowthank.htm.

Chapter 3: Fasting

1. Richard Foster, *A Celebration of Discipline* (San Francisco: Harper & Row, 1988), 47.

2. This definition is adapted from the definition given by Bruce Wilkinson in *Set Apart: Discovering Personal Victory Through Holiness* (Sisters, OR: Multnomah Publishers, 1998, 2003), 228. In my book, *Fasting: Spiritual Freedom Beyond Our Appetites* (Downers Grove, IL: InterVarsity Press, 2006), I discuss the components of this definition on pages 28–31.

3. Scot McKnight, *Fasting: The Ancient Practices* (Nashville: Thomas Nelson, 2009).

4. Thomas Ryan, *The Sacred Art of Fasting* (Woodstock, VT: Skylight Paths Publishing, 2005), 52.

5. Derek Prince, *Shaping History through Prayer and Fasting* (Springdale, PA.: Whitaker House, 1973), 185–98.

6. To learn about the Thirty Hour Famine, see http://www.30hourfamine.org/. The thirty hour famine has been adopted in many different countries. The version in New Zealand and Australia lasts forty hours. See: http://www.worldvision.com.au/40HourFamine.aspx and http://www.famine.org.nz/

Chapter 4: Contemplative Prayer

1. M. Robert Mulholland, Jr. "Prayer as Availability to God." *Weavings*, XII, no. 5 (September/October 1997), 20–26.

2. A variety of articles about *examen* can be found here: http://ignatianspirituality.com/ignatian-prayer/the-examen/.

3. Adele Ahlberg Calhoun, *Spiritual Disciplines Handbook* (Downers Grove, IL: InterVarsity Press, 2005), 209.

4. Ibid.

5. In 2006, a twentieth anniversary edition of *Open Mind, Open Heart* by Thomas Keating was published by Continuum, with updated language, a new preface, and an expanded glossary.

Chapter 5: Contemplative Approaches to Scripture

1. Michael Casey, *Sacred Reading: The Ancient Art of Lectio Divina* (Liguori, MI: Triumph, 1996), 62.

2. The material about the steps involved in Ignatian Gospel Contemplation comes from Geoff New, "Back to the Future: The Impact of the Ancient Disciplines of *Lectio Divina* and Ignatian Gospel Contemplation on Contemporary Preaching" (DMin thesis, Australian College of Theology, 2011), 34–36.

3. Ibid., 35.

4. This quotation is from an unpublished interview of Mary Ellen Ashcroft by Kimberlee Conway Ireton, July 2002. Ashcroft, an Episcopal priest, is the retreat director at Windcradle Retreat Center in Minnesota and author of numerous books. Used with permission of Kimberlee Conway Ireton and Mary Ellen Ashcroft.

Chapter 6: Hospitality

1. Henri Nouwen, *Reaching Out: The Three Movements of the Spiritual Life* (Glasgow: William Collins, 1976), 68–69.

2. I wrote a book on the ways that congregations express their identity and values through various forms of communication, including brochures and Web sites. The book is titled *Reaching Out in a Networked World: Expressing Your Congregation's Heart and Soul* (Bethesda, MD: The Alban Institute, 2008).

3. Henry G. Brinton, *The Welcoming Congregation: Roots and Fruits of Christian Hospitality* (Louisville, KY: Westminster John Knox Press, 2012), 25–26.

4. Christine D. Pohl, *Making Room: Recovering Hospitality as a Christian Tradition* (Grand Rapids: Eerdmans, 1999), 9.

5. Ibid.

Chapter 8: Spiritual Practices and Congregational Discernment

1. Ignatius of Loyola developed a rich and robust body of material on discernment. His wisdom on the subject is well worth further study, and the books about Ignatius listed at the end of chapter 5 are a good place to start. However, for the purposes of our focus, his counsel on engaging the Scriptures through contemplation provides a very good start for a congregation beginning to explore corporate discernment.

2. From the World Union for Progressive Judaism Shabbat Evening Service, available at http://wupj.org/Assets/Brochures/ShabbatService.pdf.

3. Martin B. Copenhaver. "Decide or Discern," *The Christian Century* (December 28, 2010), 31.

Chapter 9: Are Spiritual Practices Legalistic? Are They a Form of Self-Help?

1. William H. Willimon, "Too Much Practice," *The Christian Century* (March 9, 2010), 24.

2. William H. Willimon and Stanley Hauerwas, *Resident Aliens: Life in the Christian Colony* (Nashville: Abingdon Press, 1989); and William H. Willimon and Stanley Hauerwas, *Where Resident Aliens Live: Exercises for Christian Practice* (Nashville: Abingdon Press, 1996).

3. William H. Willimon, "Too Much Practice," 22.

4. Ibid., 24.

5. Ibid., 25.

6. William H. Willimon, "Impractical Christianity: Why Salvation in Jesus Christ Is Better than a Practice,"

in *A Spiritual Life: Perspectives from Poets, Prophets, and Preachers,* ed. Allan Hugh Cole Jr., 223–30 (Louisville, KY: Westminster John Knox Press, 2011).

7. Ibid., 227.

8. Ibid., 225.

9. Adele Ahlberg Calhoun, *Spiritual Disciplines Handbook* (Downers Grove, IL: InterVarsity Press, 2005), 17.

10. Willimon, "Too Much Practice," 25.

11. Richard J. Foster and Gayle D. Beebe, *Longing for God: Seven Paths of Christian Devotion* (Downers Grove, IL: InterVarsity Press, 2009), 97.

12. Ibid.

13. William H. Willimon, "Letters," *The Christian Century* (May 18, 2010), 44.

14. Donald Blosser, "Letters," *The Christian Century* (May 18, 2010), 6. Ellipsis in original.

Chapter 10: Receptivity: The Gift of Spiritual Practices

1. Sarah Bessey, "In Which I Write a Letter to Women's Ministry," The Intersections of a Spirit-Filled Life, blog, accessed at http://www.emergingmummy.com/2011/10/in-which-i-write-letter-to-womens.html. Emphases in bold are from the original blog post.

CPSIA information can be obtained at www.ICGtesting.com
Printed in the USA
LVOW080447290912

300786LV00001B/30/P